"Keeping authors and publishers updated on the complicated, always-changing aspects of literary law is a dirty job, but Tonya Evans manages to do it – and she does it well. Here is a wealth of valuable information in a concise, well-organized package. Don't sign a contract without it!"

—Jim Barnes, Managing Editor
Independent Publisher Online/Jenkins Group
www.independentpublisher.com

"The *Literary Law Guide for Authors* is a well-written, thorough, and straightforward guide that breaks down complicated legal concepts and presents them in a way that the non-lawyer can appreciate. I strongly recommend this book to anyone who needs the basic facts about copyright and trademark law and contracts."

—Ken Shropshire, Esquire
Entertainment lawyer and professor,
University of Pennsylvania

"This book covers every phase of the writing and publishing process. Thankfully, it does so with clarity and reader-friendliness. For ease in use, key symbols highlight interesting information such as myths, questions, legal notes, checklists, etc. A great tool for every writer's bookshelf."

—Marilyn Ross
Cofounder of SPAN and coauthor of *Complete Guide to Self-Publishing* and *Jump Start Your Book Sales*

"Not only does this book address our most fervent copyright questions, but it eloquently covers privacy issues, right of publicity, and trademark law, and it provides sample contracts and legal forms. This is an easy read, but it is also a valuable reference book. I found the glossary complete and helpful. There is an extremely informative table of contents, and the index is top notch."

—Patricia Fry
President of SPAWN

"The well-crafted layout, complete with helpful keynotes, markers, and illustrations, simplifies the often-intimidating paragraphs of lawyer-speak. The detail given to the whys and where-fores of contracts and agreements brings new insight to the potential for liability and protracted entanglements when one ignores the fine print. . . . This guide ushers the reader through the changing landscape and legislation surrounding the written word. The enclosed CD offers adaptable templates for most every situation. Keep this one next to your dictionary!"

—*Midwest Book Review*

"The most often asked questions that I receive from aspiring authors involve the complicated language in a publishing contract. Now I direct them to the *Literary Law Guide for Authors*."

—Max Rodriguez
Publisher and Editor of *QBR The Black Book Review*

(this page is intentionally blank—this type does NOT print)

Literary Law Guide for Authors

Copyright, Trademark, and Contracts in Plain Language

Second Edition

Tonya M. Evans
with a foreword by Dan Poynter

Literary Entrepreneur Series™

FYOS Entertainment, LLC
Philadelphia

Publisher's Cataloging-in-Publication

    Evans, Tonya Marie.
      Literary law guide for authors : copyright,
    trademark, and contracts in plain language / Tonya M.
    Evans ; with foreword by Dan Poynter. — 2nd ed.
      p. cm.
      Includes index.
      LCCN 2002092370
      ISBN 9780-9674579-7-1

      1. Authors—Legal status, laws, etc.—United States—
    Popular works. 2. Authors and publishers—United States
    —Popular works. 3. Copyright—United States—Popular
    works. 4. Trademarks—United States—Popular works.
    I. Title.

    KF390.A96E93 2005   343.73'0780705

                    QBI04-200476

Request for permission to reproduce any portion of this book
should be addressed to:

FYOS Entertainment, LLC
ATTN: Permissions Department
P.O. Box 25216
Philadelphia, PA 19119

LE Series™ Books and logo, FYOS® and logo, and the title and
trade dress of the *Literary Law Guide for Authors* are the intellectual
property of FYOS Entertainment, LLC.

Editing by Lisa A. Smith, Writing at Work
Interior design by Rob Roehrick, Roehrick Design
Cover design by James Jones

31019154048923

I dedicate this book to the memory and indomitable spirit of my grandfather William Sutton Borden Sr. (Pop Pop), who endowed me with the same entrepreneurial mind-set that led to the success of countless legendary family businesses and with an abiding appreciation of literature and reading.

Contents

(this page is intentionally blank—this type does NOT print)

Foreword

I remember when I first met Tonya and her mother, Susan Evans, co-author of the first edition of this book. While attending the 2001 BookExpo America in Chicago, Illinois, I was walking through the Small Press area, as I do every year. Suddenly I heard someone call out, "Mr. Poynter, Mr. Poynter!" I turned to be greeted by Tonya. She introduced herself, escorted me to her booth, and told me about her new publishing company and about how instrumental my book, *The Self-Publishing Manual*, had been for her. At that time I also met her mother, Susan. As we spoke, I marveled at their energy and vision. And I took great pride in meeting yet another family-owned publishing company destined for success.

Tonya and Susan prove that the new publishing model works if you put your plans into motion. That momentum can move you forward to achieve great success in the publishing industry. Tonya and Susan take this momentum even farther by using their expertise in intellectual property and publishing law in a new series of law-related guides. *The Literary Law Guide for Authors*, first in the series, contains information desperately needed by authors and publishers alike. Few attorneys devote their practice to publishing law and intellectual property. Fewer still understand the law from the perspectives of attorney, writer, and publisher, as do these dedicated legal eagles.

I was prompted to write *The Self-Publishing Manual* because so many authors wanted to know how to successfully self-publish their work. Tonya and Susan were moved by the same force – a demand for more information – to create this indispensable guidebook.

Since 1969, when I created my publishing company, Para Publishing, I have seen the number of self-published authors increase astronomically. The success of self-published authors, and other independent publishers, has much to do with technological advances that make it more economical to publish in shorter runs. But with all the blessings of self-publishing, not the least of which is creative and business control, come the burdens of managing the legalities of writing.

All too often, writers who tend carefully to the creative aspects of their craft do not give the same level of attention to the legal concepts and laws related to it, such as copyright, trademark, constitutional law, and contracts. Whether knowledgeable or not, however, writers are directly affected by these concepts and laws. More than that, writers are responsible for knowing how to protect their work and how to avoid breaking the law in the process. As Tonya so aptly notes, what you don't know about the law as it relates to writing and publishing can hurt you.

The *Literary Law Guide for Authors* is a timely, well-written, and authoritative layperson's guide to understanding complicated legal concepts. It offers straightforward explanations and relevant examples based on the publishing industry. Most importantly, the fact that lawyers wrote it adds a high level of legitimacy to the information provided.

You will undoubtedly refer to the *Literary Law Guide for Authors* at every phase of the writing and publishing process. From the chapter on copyright to the valuable forms contained in the appendix and on the companion CD-ROM, each section addresses your most basic and pressing questions in a way that you will easily understand. Tonya makes it possible for you to quickly learn what you need to know about publishing law and intellectual property.

I highly recommend this book to those who want to know more about the legal side of writing. You cannot be a successful author and publisher without effectively traversing the law as it relates to the publishing industry. The *Literary Law Guide* is your indispensable road map. Happy travels!

Dan Poynter
The Self-Publishing Manual
http://ParaPublishing.com

Preface to the Second Edition

A legal reference guide is only as good as the timeliness and relevance of the information it contains. This is particularly true in the case of intellectual property and literary law because each year new court rulings and legislative amendments emerge to address the technological and other advances that make it both easier and more difficult for writers to publish and protect their work, and to make a living in the process. That's why I am committed to keeping this book up to date with new editions – so that you always have the best information available.

In the first edition, co-authored with Susan Borden Evans, my mother, we set out to empower writers by covering the complex areas of copyright, trademark, and publishing law contracts in a user-friendly, effective, and informative way. And based on the response we received from writers and industry professionals, we succeeded in providing much needed information to dispel long-held myths that often left writers vulnerable and confused; and we succeeded in making difficult topics easier to understand and to use to your advantage. In fact, the first edition was honored as a finalist in both the Publishers Marketing Association 2004 Benjamin Franklin Awards and the Independent Publisher Online's "IPPY" 2004 Awards.

In this second edition, I use the foundation that my mother and I laid in the first edition to enhance existing information and add new information. I based my revisions on the wonderful questions we've received since 2003; on cases like Tasini and *National Geographic* that apply to a magazine or newspaper publisher's right to use freelance in-print works in electronic editions, and the Rosetta Books case that deals with electronic rights in the trade publishing industry and the definition of "book" now that e-books are here to stay; and on new and pending legislation that affects authors.

This edition includes new and expanded information on

- electronic rights
- reclaiming your copyright
- fair use, permissions, and work made for hire
- the difference between fair use and public domain

- how to refer to real people and places in your work
- writers and trademarks
- the most recent changes in copyright and trademark laws
- pending and new legislation affecting writers

This second edition also includes an updated glossary and more than a dozen new and updated publishing industry forms set out in the appendix of forms and in .pdf format on the CD-ROM that accompanies the book.

This legal reference guide will help you to increase your knowledge about your intellectual property and contractual rights as a writer, to learn more about how to use other people's words and other copyrighted works legally in your own work, and to better understand and learn how to protect and increase the value of your electronic rights in the twenty-first century.

Preface to the First edition

Wide-eyed and full of ambition, in 1999 we undertook the task of transforming the raw manuscript of Tonya's poetry into a published book, *Seasons of Her*, which now graces the shelves of bookstores across the country. At first, however, the books, housed in dozens of boxes, graced only the floor of our living room. We quickly discovered that we had a lot to learn about the publishing industry.

Our first step in overcoming a mountain of information was to compile a list of writer's conferences, organizations, Web sites, and magazines (see Appendix A). We found our way to Black Writers Alliance (BWA), Publishers Marketing Association (PMA), and *The Self-Publishing Manual* by Dan Poynter, the guru of independent publishers.

We scoured the pages of *The Self-Publishing Manual* and spent hours surfing the Web sites of various organizations. Quickly, we learned that there is strength in numbers, especially when those numbers consist of a network of like-minded people who are open to sharing information and supporting one another. We learned that the BWA was hosting a conference in Atlanta. Without ever laying eyes on any of the members or organizers, but feeling a real sense of camaraderie with her online writer's group, Tonya convinced Susan to buy plane tickets and reserve a hotel room at the conference. Tonya was also invited to perform her poetry at the Friday night poetry event. "What a great way to meet the group in person!" Tonya thought. So on that Friday, we packed our babies (aka our books), checked in for our flight, and checked our baggage (including our babies). We asked the skycap to take good care of them. He said he would. He lied.

Murphy's Law was in full effect on that fateful Friday. A flight delay made us so late we were afraid we would miss the poetry event. We thought that was bad enough. We thought wrong. The worst part was that our babies did not arrive at all that day. Of course anyone who has attended similar conferences knows how important it is to have your books with you to display and sell. So we learned Literary Entrepreneur Rule #1: *Never* check your babies.

Luckily, we made it to the poetry event just in time to hear Tonya's name called as the next performer. The next day, Susan had one of those sixth-sense feelings that only mothers have. She decided we should return to the airport to find the lost bag. And there, in the middle of the lost baggage claim area, all by itself, sat the bag, as if it had been waiting for us all along.

After that experience, we knew things would only get better; and they did. We attended seminars, gathered information, and asked questions; our eyes were opened to a whole new world. We learned the business as writers and publishers from the ground up. We then set out to teach others by using our critical thinking skills and legal knowledge.

That conference changed our lives forever. Established members of the publishing industry taught us information critical to making it in the business. We gathered pages and pages of information that we reviewed, discussed, and condensed into a business plan for our publishing company, FYOS Entertainment, LLC. We had so much to absorb and to prepare for that we didn't mind when our return flight was delayed on the tarmac for hours. We pretended we were on Air Force One planning our next great mission. And we were!

In that planning session, we agreed to embark on an ambitious venture: a series of seminars to educate writers about topics of interest within the publishing industry. Our ultimate goal was to create a group of literary services that would go beyond publishing and that would turn writers into Literary Entrepreneurs. To complete this mission we would capitalize on our unique position as writers, publishers, and attorneys. We turned our plan into action that fall when we partnered with Xlibris (we had met one of their reps at the conference) to co-host our first seminar titled New Technologies in the Literary Industry.

Another step in our mission was to write a series of books for Literary Entrepreneurs. This proved to be a lofty goal because we are so different, and we are, after all, mother and daughter. Tonya, the daughter, is a planner who is organized, detail oriented, focused, and driven (okay, she's the taskmaster). Susan, the mother, is a big-picture person who loves short-term projects with definite deadlines, and she often (read *always*) works up to the very last minute, much to Tonya's chagrin. Thankfully, these differences complement each other wonderfully well. For this first book in the series, Tonya focused on copyright and contracts, Susan concentrated on trademarks, and together they fine-tuned the entire project.

The synergy of opposite energies works because we are both committed to the overall goal of educating Literary Entrepreneurs and, in the process, building a strong family business that will last for years to come. With our seminar series, this book, and our plans for future Literary Entrepreneur Series™ publications, we are well on our way; and so are you.

15

(this page is intentionally blank—this type does NOT print)

Symbol Key

When you see this symbol . . .   It means . . .

 Myth: Presents, examines, and dispels a common myth.

 Note: Draws your attention to a particular topic of interest.

 Question: Presents and answers a frequently asked question.

 Checklist: Lists several items to consider on a particular topic.

 Legal Note: Examines the facts and disposition of a leading case, or the status of a statute or pending legislation.

 Contract Clause: Presents a key contract clause to be considered.

 Form: Provides the applicable form in Appendix B and on the CD-ROM.

 Illustration or Example: Illustrates a particular issue to clarify an important point.

(this page is intentionally blank—this type does NOT print)

From Writer to Literary Entrepreneur

Chapter 1

We writers, like other artists and creative people, are notorious for getting caught up in the process of creating, often at the expense of fully comprehending and appreciating the business side of writing. We want to create the next great work of fiction, the most referred to reference guide, the most profound poem, the most telling memoir, the wittiest article or short story or essay. To the writer, mastering the craft of writing in order to complete the manuscript and publish the work is often the sole objective.

These goals, quite obviously, are critical because if we do not nurture and attend to the work during its creation, there is little reason to engage in the process at all. Because of our absorption in the writing, however, little attention is given to the potential legalities we writers face before, during, and after the creative process.

Think for a moment about the countless hours you have already spent (and continue to spend) writing, typing, editing, reading, and critiquing — and writing, typing, editing, reading, and critiquing again. You have undoubtedly attended dozens of writers' conferences; perhaps you've taken writing courses and perused innumerable how-to books on writing, editing, style, and publishing. You have poured over the comments written by family and friends after you've circulated your manuscript for the umpteenth time. And there is no doubt that you have done all of these things with the hope of creating the perfect manuscript, of completing your lifelong dream to publish your work.

While you were hunched over your computer or desk writing the next great literary work, did you ever stop to consider the legal implications, rights, and obligations that may exist because of the words you wrote?

When you completed your first novel, poem, or essay, did you stand guard over the stack of pages or the diskette that held your life's passion, forbidding anyone to see your manuscript for fear that they might steal your brilliant ideas? Or worse, did you fall victim to the myth that if you mailed your manuscript to yourself, your copyright interests were somehow protected?

Have you ever mentioned the name of a famous (or not-so-famous but just as real) person in your writing and wondered, if only for a moment, whether it was illegal to do so?

Do you think you should patent the name of your company, trademark your book, and copyright your invention? In other words, are you confused about which term correctly applies to which type of intellectual property and how the three types can, in fact, interrelate under certain circumstances?

Do you hope to sign a publishing contract but lack the knowledge to discuss the basic terms, rights, and obligations with your legal representative, publisher, or agent?

If the answer to any of these questions is yes, then you are reading the right book. This guide gives you the facts about the nature of copyright and trademark, how to protect your intellectual property and other rights, and how to avoid the illegal use of intellectual property belonging to others.

In short, the *Literary Law Guide for Authors* gives you the information about your legal rights and potential pitfalls in plain language, and provides a comprehensive reference list of other resources. Within these pages you will find real-life examples and illustrations for easy application. In plain language, I present the basic copyright and trademark laws as of the date of publication of this second edition, basic contract terms, and things to consider before signing on the dotted line. Also, I provide important and necessary forms in this book and on the companion CD. Once you have digested the information here, contact an attorney who specializes in publishing law or intellectual property to see how the general principles I explain may apply to your particular situation. This last bit of advice is most important. Do not use this guide in place of legal counsel by a lawyer knowledgeable in publishing law and intellectual property.

The Name Game: Copyright, Trademark, or Patent?

No one word is more misused or more misunderstood by writers than the word "copyright." This single word creates such confusion and lends itself to so much misinformation because rumors, assumptions, and complicated changes in the law make it difficult for writers to separate fact from fiction. But because copyright consists of such a valuable bundle of rights, it is imperative that writers fully comprehend the nature of copyright and the process by which it is protected.

Writers are not the only ones confused by the word "copyright." More than a few business-savvy agents, publishers, and even attorneys, who are in the business of negotiating rights, have a woefully inadequate understanding of the nature of copyright. This is particularly troublesome because writers trust these industry professionals to protect their interests; the explanation that "it's always done this way" is simply not good enough when valuable rights are at stake. For you to successfully protect your copyrights and enjoy lucrative financial benefits from successful negotiations to license and sell your rights, you must first understand for yourself how copyright is created and protected.

What you don't know about intellectual property ownership can jeopardize your rights and potentially expose you to legal liability. So let's take a closer look at the differences between the various types of intellectual property.

Copyright: A copyright protects an author's original artistic or literary work, whether published or unpublished. Under copyright law, the term "author" has a special meaning: the creator of an original literary or artistic work. Thus, the word "author" includes not only writers but photographers, singers, painters, sculptors – anyone who creates a literary or artistic work. Examples of literary and artistic works include manuscripts, book covers, song lyrics, sheet music, musical scores, paintings, sketches, sound recordings (music), films, and photographs. And those lists are not all-inclusive.

Trademark: A trademark protects a word, phrase, symbol, or device – the mark – used in business (referred to in the law as commerce) to identify and distinguish one product from another. For example, HarperCollins® is a registered trademark for fiction and nonfiction books, calendars, posters, address books, appointment books, and diaries.

Service Mark: A service mark protects a word, phrase, symbol, or device – again, the mark – used in business to identify and distinguish one service from another. For example, iUniverse® is a registered service mark for the publication of books and electronic publishing services, including the publication of text and graphic works of others on CD-ROMs and in digital formats; iUniverse features new authors, out-of-print works, educational titles, and college course materials – all on a wide variety of subjects.

Patent: The patent is probably the least used intellectual property in the publishing industry. A patent protects an invention by granting the inventor the right to exclude others from producing or using the inventor's discovery or invention for a specific period of time. Some examples of patentable inventions include the talking book, an e-book reader, a typewriter, and an Internet-based customer referral system such as that used by Amazon.com.

> In some instances, patent, copyright, and trademark protection are all available for a single product. For example:
>
> ABC Company has developed a unique method for attaching CDs to the inside back cover of its books; the technique is an advance in the industry. ABC can seek a patent for this novel invention. A copyright exists in the songs on the CD and in the book itself, and those copyrights can be registered. ABC can also seek to register a trademark for this unique book-CD combination, which the company will market as MUSIQUEBOOK™.

21

An Overview of Literary Law Questions

Authors are, by nature, an inquisitive bunch. Over the years they have asked me many questions about writing and the law. I answer the most important ones in depth in this book. Here's a brief rundown of what you will learn.

What can and cannot be copyrighted? Generally, copyright protects all original writing: letters, e-mail, poetry, fiction, nonfiction, and songs. Book titles cannot be copyrighted. Ideas cannot be copyrighted. As noted earlier, copyright also protects other kinds of creative work, such as photographs, CDs, recordings of written works, musical scores, movies, sculptures, artwork, and even architecture. For more information, see chapters 2 and 3.

What do you have to do to copyright your work? If you have created an original work in some tangible form – in writing or on film or tape or canvas, for example – then you don't have to do anything. You automatically own your copyright. But you should register it for further protection. For more information, see chapter 2.

How much can you quote without permission? Contrary to popular belief, there is no set number of words you can use under the fair use doctrine. A related question is whether an author needs permission to quote from phone calls, in-person interviews, e-mail, letters, the newspaper, a TV commercial, or a company slogan. The answer will not be satisfying because it is a lawyerly one: it depends. These ever-popular questions are dealt with in chapter 4.

Another often-asked question is whether you can use a picture you took of someone else in any way you choose. This question involves balancing the copyright interest in the photograph with the legal concept known as right of publicity. Although the photographer usually owns the copyright in the picture, the person captured in the picture holds a competing interest: the right of publicity. This right, governed by state law, gives a person (usually a celebrity or public figure) the exclusive right to use his or her name, likeness, or other aspect of his or her persona, and the right to prevent others from using those aspects without authorization. For more details, see chapter 6. Similarly, the photographer may even be prohibited from making and distributing copies of a picture that captures a painting, sculpture, or other work of art if that work is otherwise protected by copyright (see chapter 4).

22

Another topic of great concern to writers is writing about real people and real businesses or organizations. Do the same rules apply when you mention your Aunt Tilly as when you mention Oprah? Is the rule the same for writing about the mom-and-pop store on the corner as for McDonald's®? Do the rules change if you say positive things as opposed to negative (but true) things? These questions involve the rights of publicity and privacy, as well as trademark law, and are explored in chapters 6 through 9.

Writers also ask about trademarks and service marks. A common question is: When should the ™ symbol be used, and when is it proper to use the ® symbol? As soon as you have a mark you want to claim trademark rights in, you can use the ™ symbol; you don't need permission to do that. But the ® symbol can be used only after a mark is registered. Authors also want to know about the benefits of trademark registration and whether they can trademark a pen name, character, domain name, or book title. Generally speaking, you cannot trademark a pen name or the title of a single book. But you may be able to register the title of a series of books (e.g., Chicken Soup for the Soul®). For characters, trademark protection depends on whether they are associated with the sale of goods (e.g., Mickey Mouse®). You can also register a domain name if it identifies goods or a service (e.g., Amazon.com® or iUniverse.com®). For more information about these questions and to learn about the difference between common law trademarks, state registered trademarks, and federally registered trademarks, see chapter 7.

Another topic frequently discussed by authors is that of contract negotiations. Specifically, authors ask whether the terms are negotiable. The answer is that despite the commonly held belief perpetuated in the industry, everything is negotiable, and all terms should be discussed before you sign on the dotted line. For more information about contracts as well as a discussion of the most important terms and items to consider, see chapters 12 through 14.

Since publication of the first edition of this book, writers have sent us important questions that I cover in this second edition. For example, many writers wanted to know whether registering your work with a writer's guild is the same as registering with the Copyright Office.

Contrary to popular belief, registering your work with a writer's guild or organization does not constitute registration under copyright law unless (1) the guild or organization specifically states otherwise and (2) it provides you with a registration certificate from the Copyright Office. In fact, you should register your copyright before submitting it to anyone or to any organization. Organizations like the Writer's Guild of America allow writers to archive their scripts in the organization's database, which the organization refers to as "registration." Although archiving your work with a guild or organization may be beneficial in certain writing genres as evidence within that circle that your work existed on a certain date and is available to be developed, guild and organization registration should never replace registering your copyright with the Copyright Office at the Library of Congress. Proper copyright registration procedures are covered in chapter 2.

23

Writers also frequently ask, when is the right time to register your copyright? This is a good question and one that does not necessarily have a precise answer. The lawyerly answer is based on the benefits of timely registration defined in the Copyright Act: you should register before your work is infringed and within three months of publication. This advice is not exactly helpful because (1) you certainly cannot predict when your work might be infringed, and (2) some work is never published. I cover this issue in greater detail in chapter 2.

With all of that said, welcome to the complex and often confusing world of literary law. My goal is to simplify it for you and to help you have a better understanding of your legal rights and responsibilities as a Literary Entrepreneur.

Copyright Chapter 2

Copyright law protects your exclusive right to exploit (use productively) your original work. Copyright law was written to encourage the free exchange of ideas and to stimulate the progress of "useful arts," which benefit society. The theory behind the law is that the progress of useful arts is in the best interest of society but that creative individuals will not freely share their work without some say over how it is used. (To learn more about the history of copyright, see chapter 10.)

The federal Copyright Act provides copyright protection to "authors" (creators) of "original works." The act covers literary, dramatic, musical, artistic, and certain other works of an intellectual nature. Copyright protection is available for both published works (those made available to the public) and unpublished works (those shared with only a few or not at all).

Protecting Ideas

The Copyright Act expressly excludes ideas from its protection. *The American Heritage Dictionary* defines "idea" as "something, such as a thought or conception that potentially or actually exists in the mind as a product of mental activity." Therefore, the idea of writing a book about, for instance, a falsely accused prisoner who escapes from jail to prove his innocence and find the real killer cannot be protected under the Copyright Act. But the act does protect a written manuscript based on that idea. This conclusion makes sense in light of the way copyright is created. Copyright protection exists the moment an artistic or literary expression is fixed in a tangible form. Until an idea is fixed in a writing or recording, it is just that – an idea. Once fixed in a tangible form, the creative expression (assuming, of course, that it is also original) is protected by copyright.

25

It is not correct, however, to assume that an idea can never be protected. In fact, the protection of ideas is critical in situations where, for instance, you submit a book proposal to a publisher, pitch a screenplay to a producer or studio, or brainstorm with a collaborator about potential story lines. In such situations, ideas may be protectable under state law related to theories of contract, property, or in some cases, misappropriation.

When Copyright Ownership Begins

Copyright exists automatically when a work is created. For the purposes of copyright law, a work is created when it is fixed in a copy or phonorecord for the first time. By "copy" the law means material objects – such as books, manuscripts, electronic files, Web sites, e-mail, sheet music, musical scores, film, videotape, or microfilm – from which a work can be read or visually perceived either directly or with the aid of a machine or device. Phonorecords are material objects – such as cassette tapes, CDs, or LPs, but not motion picture soundtracks on which sounds are recorded and which combine moving images and sound. Thus, for example, a song (the work) can be fixed in sheet music (copies) or in a CD (phonorecord) or both. If a work is created over a period of time, the copyright applies automatically to whatever part is fixed on a particular date. So as soon as you write the first two paragraphs of your book, whether by hand on paper or by keying them into a computer, those paragraphs are immediately and automatically copyrighted – even if you don't get around to writing the third paragraph until a week or a year later.

> Copyright protection is not available for any work of the United States government (for example, any publication created by a governmental agency, like the Copyright Office), but the United States government may receive and hold copyrights transferred to it by assignment, bequest, or otherwise.

Showing the World That You Own Your Work

To demonstrate to the world that you own your work, you should use a copyright notice. The notice should contain all of the following three elements:

☑ **The symbol**, which for printed material is the letter "C" in a circle – ©; or, for CDs, audio tapes, and LPs, the letter "P" in a circle – ℗. Instead of the symbol you may use the word "Copyright" or the abbreviation "Copr."

☑ **The year** in which the work is first published. If your work is a compilation or a derivative that includes previously published material, use the year in which you first publish it. If your work consists of a picture, graphic, or sculpture, with or without accompanying text, and it is reproduced on greeting cards, postcards, stationery, jewelry, dolls, toys, or any useful article, no date is necessary. If your work is unpublished, use the year of creation and the phrase "Unpublished work" before the copyright symbol in the notice.

☑ **The name** of the copyright owner. (If you're writing under a pseudonym, see page 51.)

The copyright statement would then look like this: **© 2005 by Patsi Pen**

Note that if your work is unpublished but copies leave your control, your notice should look like this: **Unpublished work. © 2005 by Patsi Pen**

You should also consider including the phrase "All rights reserved". This phrase lets the public know that you have reserved each right in the bundle of rights that copyright contains. In that case, the copyright statement would look like this:

© 2005 by Patsi Pen
All rights reserved

Although use of the copyright notice is no longer required by law, it is still important that it appear in all copyrighted works because it informs the public that the work is protected by copyright, identifies the copyright owner, and shows the year of first publication. Copyright notice is still required by law, however, for works that were published before 1989 (see chapter 10). Furthermore, if your copyright is infringed and a proper notice of copyright appears on the published copy to which the infringer had access, then he or she cannot argue that the infringement was innocent. Innocent infringement can occur only when the infringer did not realize that the work was protected. (See chapter 5.)

 The copyright owner has the responsibility to use the copyright notice and doesn't need anyone's permission to use it. The copyright owner can use the notice without registering with the Copyright Office.

What a Copyright Owner Has the Right to Do

In general, the Copyright Act gives a copyright owner the exclusive right to do and to authorize others to do (or preclude others from doing) the following:

☑ Reproduce the work (make copies)

☑ Prepare derivative works based on the original (create a motion picture based on a novel or a novel based on a motion picture)

☑ Distribute copies of the work to the public (publish) by sale or other transfer of ownership, or by rental, lease, or lending

☑ Perform the work publicly (a public reading)

☑ Display the work publicly (hang a painting in an art gallery)

☑ Perform the work publicly by means of a digital audio transmission (DAT), in the case of sound recordings

Collectively, these rights are often referred to as an author's exclusive bundle of rights.

27

???? Without the copyright symbol on my manuscript, I won't have any copyright protection.

This is false. In 1989, the United States joined the Berne Convention for the Protection of Literary and Artistic Works, which is an international copyright treaty that requires all member countries to eliminate formal requirements as a condition to copyright protection. As a result, you do not have to use the copyright symbol or notice, or even register your copyright with the Copyright Office in order to create a protectable copyright interest. Copyright in original works of author-ship exists as soon as the work is fixed in a tangible form.

Scope of Copyright Protection

The Copyright Act protects only original works fixed in a tangible medium of expression now known or later developed, from which they can be perceived, reproduced, or otherwise communicated, either directly or with the aid of a machine or device. Works of authorship include the following categories:

☑ Literary works

☑ Musical works, including any accompanying words

☑ Dramatic works, including any accompanying music

☑ Pantomimes and choreographic works

☑ Pictorial, graphic, and sculptural works

☑ Motion pictures and other audiovisual works

☑ Sound recordings

☑ Architectural works

28

The Elements of Copyrightable Works

Originality: Copyrightable works must be original; that is, the work (story, song, poem, drawing, movie, and so forth) must be of the author's own creation. The originality requirement has a low threshold and does not require novelty, ingenuity, or any particular quality.

Fixation: An author's creation must be fixed in a tangible medium of expression. For instance, copyright does not exist until a story is written, typed, or recorded. The fixation may be viewed by way of a machine such as a computer, projector, digital camera, scanner, or even a machine that has not yet been created. But an idea, procedure, process, system, method of operation, concept, principle, or discovery is not protectable by copyright. Also, a live performance that is not fixed in a tangible form (written or recorded) is not protected by copyright law. So it's a good idea to write out or tape record a speech before you give it. But simultaneous fixation, such as a live broadcast of a sporting event, is protected by copyright.

? Neo Pro, Inc., hosts a weekly performance as part of its Neo Pro Performance Series℠. At these live neosoul performances, the renowned poet Flow performs original poetry from her book *Flow's Show* with a live band; the performance by Flow and the band was previously recorded by her producer, Mr. Soul Explosion. Has a copyright been created in Flow's poetry? In Mr. Soul Explosion's music? How does the live performance factor into the equation?

Answer: Flow's poetry is copyrighted because it is both *original* and *fixed* as a writing in her book. The music of Mr. Soul Explosion is copyrighted because it is *original* and previously recorded, thus *fixed* in a tangible expression. Additionally, both Flow and Mr. Soul Explosion have the right to engage in the live performance of their copyrighted work.

What Copyright Does Not Protect

Despite the broad protection of copyright law, it does not protect the following things:

☑ Works that have not been fixed in a tangible form of expression (for example, choreographic works that have not been notated or recorded, or improvisational speeches or performances that have not been written or recorded)

☑ Titles, names, short phrases, and slogans; familiar symbols or designs; mere variations of typographic ornamentation, lettering, or coloring; mere listings of ingredients or contents

☑ Ideas, procedures, methods, systems, processes, concepts, principles, discoveries, or devices, as distinguished from a description, explanation, or illustration

☑ Works consisting entirely of information that is common property and containing no original authorship (for example: standard calendars, height and weight charts, tape measures and rulers, and lists or tables taken from public documents or other common sources)

29

Copyright Registration

Registration of your copyright creates a public record of the facts and circumstances pertaining to it. While registration is not necessary for copyright protection, the Copyright Act gives you certain advantages under the law if you do register your work.

The Copyright Office ordinarily does not compare copyright registration forms with existing deposit copies or registration records to determine whether works submitted for registration are similar to any material for which a registration of a copyright claim already exists. Therefore, the records of the Copyright Office may contain any number of registrations for works describing or illustrating the same underlying idea, method, or system.

Advantages of Copyright Registration

☑ You can file an infringement suit only if the copyright is registered.

☑ If obtained before or within five years of publication, registration establishes sufficient (prima facie) evidence in court of the validity of the copyright and of the facts stated in the registration certificate.

☑ If you register within three months after publication of the work or prior to an infringement, the defendant is required to prove that infringement does not exist. This is a critical advantage because ordinarily the person who files a lawsuit has to prove his or her case; but if you have registered your copyright in a timely manner, then the burden of proof falls to the defendant. This is known as burden shifting.

☑ If registration is made within three months after publication of the work or prior to an infringement, statutory damages and attorney's fees will be available to the copyright owner in court actions. Otherwise, only an award of actual damages and profits is available.

☑ Registration allows the copyright owner to record the registration with the U. S. Customs Service for protection against the importation of infringing copies.

? As a United States citizen, can I protect my copyright outside of the United States?

Answer: There is no such thing as an international copyright that will protect your work in every country. Each country has its own copyright laws. Nonetheless, most countries do offer foreign works some protection against infringement based in large part on certain international treaties and conventions (see chapter 10).

How to Register: For the original registration of your book, manuscript, poetry, other text, or other artistic work, send an application form, a nonrefundable filing fee ($30 as of this writing) for each application, and one or more nonreturnable samples of the work being registered to the Copyright Office. All three items should be submitted in the same package; an incomplete submission will not be processed and may be returned. You can contact the Copyright Office for specific deposit requirements, which means what kind and how many physical copies of your particular work the Copyright Office will require for review. Deposit requirements vary according to the type of work and the publication status. For contact information, see page 38 at the end of this chapter.

A Word about Delivery of Mail to the Copyright Office: Because of the events of September 11, 2001, and its aftermath, the Copyright Office implemented new guidelines for receipt of deliveries. Mail sent to the Copyright Office is now screened off-site prior to arrival on Capitol Hill. This process can add three to five days to the delivery time for all mail sent to the Copyright Office. Additionally, the Copyright Office no longer accepts on-site deliveries from commercial couriers and messengers. A message on their Web site explains: "First Class U.S. Postal Service mail is received regularly by the Library, but it is delayed for up to two weeks. Packages sent through private carriers, such as UPS and FedEx, are delayed three to five days. There is no overnight delivery to the Library."

To track your copyright application materials, send all correspondence via certified or registered mail, and request a return receipt; or send via a private carrier (but not a courier or messenger). Also, never send the only copy of your work.

[????] Mailing my manuscript to myself is as good as registering my copyright with the Library of Congress.

This myth is known as the poor man's copyright, but it does not offer any additional protection beyond that which already exists once your idea is fixed and thus your work is created. Additionally it does not constitute a registration of your copyright. See page 32 for more information.

Types of Application Forms: The following application forms, which are the most relevant for writers, are all reproduced in Appendix B and on the CD-ROM.

Form TX for published and unpublished nondramatic literary works

Form PA for published and unpublished works of the performing arts (musical and dramatic works, pantomimes and choreographic works, motion pictures and other audiovisual works)

Form SE for serials, works issued or intended to be issued in successive parts bearing numerical or chronological designations (Issue 1, 2, 3, etc. or Fall Issue, Spring Issue, etc.) and intended to be continued indefinitely (periodicals, newspapers, magazines, newsletters, annuals, journals, etc.)

Form SR for published and unpublished sound recordings

Form VA for published and unpublished works of the visual arts (pictorial, graphic, and sculptural works, including architectural works)

Effective Date: Copyright registration is effective on the date the Copyright Office receives all of the required elements in acceptable form.

Evidence of Application and Registration: If you apply for copyright registration, you will not receive an acknowledgment that your application has been received because the Copyright Office receives more than six hundred thousand applications each year. But a Copyright Office

31

staff member will call or send a letter if further information is needed. You will receive a certificate of registration in about four or five months, indicating that the work has been registered; or, if the application cannot be accepted, you will receive a letter explaining why it has been rejected.

Correcting an Error in the Original Application: To correct an error in a copyright registration or to add information, you must file a supplementary registration form – Form CA – with the Copyright Office. The current filing fee for Form CA is $100.

The Poor Man's Copyright Myth

The concept known as the poor man's copyright says basically that you should mail yourself a copy of your work and not open it in order to establish the date that your work existed in case you ever need to defend your work or challenge a work you believe infringes on your rights. Unfortunately, this pervasive myth continues to be perpetuated even by established writers, and it should be abolished from the writing world. The poor man's copyright does not offer any additional protection beyond that which already exists once your idea is fixed and thus your work is created. Additionally, it does not constitute a registration of your copyright.

A prevalent but misguided school of thought within the trade publishing industry holds that because the theft of book manuscripts occurs, in their opinion, relatively rarely, it is not necessary to go to the trouble of registering your work. But registration is easy (no need for a lawyer) and inexpensive (only $30) – a small price to pay to preserve valuable rights.

How to Investigate the Copyright Status of a Work

There are several ways to investigate whether a work is protected by copyright or whether it is in the public domain. The easiest way to begin is to examine the work for the copyright notice information, place and date of publication, and author information. The second way is to conduct a search of the Copyright Office catalog and other records either online at www.copyright.gov/records/ or in person. The third way is to have the Copyright Office conduct a search for you. In many cases you will need to use more than one way to conduct a comprehensive search, and even a comprehensive search may not be conclusive. Therefore, it may be important to contact an attorney before coming to any conclusions about your particular copyright status question.

The Copyright Office published the Catalog of Copyright Entries (CCE) in book form from 1891 to 1978 and in microfiche form from 1979 to 1982. Many libraries maintain copies of the CCE, and the CCE may be a good starting point for research. Because the CCE does not contain copyright assignment and other recorded documents, however, it cannot be the only method used to track copyright ownership conclusively. Also, while the CCE includes facts about copyright registration, it does not provide a verbatim account nor does it include contact information for the copyright claimant. Copyright registrations after 1978 are found online only, in the Internet databases of the Copyright Office.

Where to Search for Information about Registered Copyrights

The Copyright Office is in the Library of Congress James Madison Memorial Building, 101 Independence Avenue SE, Washington DC 20559-6000. Most Copyright Office records are open to public inspection and searching from 8:30 a.m. to 5:00 p.m., Eastern time, Monday through Friday, except federal holidays. The general public can conduct free searches of the card catalog, the automated catalog containing records from 1978 forward, record books, and microfilm records of assignments and related documents. Certain records, including correspondence files and deposit copies, can be accessed only by the Copyright Office itself, for a fee. You will find the Copyright Office fee schedule in Appendix B and on the CD-ROM. Be advised, however, that fees are subject to change; you can verify the actual amount of search fees at www.copyright.gov/docs/fees/.html.

The Copyright Office staff will search its records for you for a fee of $75 per hour. Based on the initial information you furnish, the office will provide an estimate of the total search fee, which you submit along with your request. The office will then proceed with the search and send you a typewritten report or, if you prefer, an oral report by telephone. In the case of search requests based on evidentiary requirements for a lawsuit, search reports can be certified on request for an extra fee of $80 per hour. Note that the search fee does not include the cost of additional certificates, photocopies of deposits, or copies of other Copyright Office records.

33

Transfer of Copyright

Any or all of the copyright owner's bundle of rights or any subdivision of those rights may be transferred to a third party. In other words, you may transfer one right in the bundle to one person or entity and another right or two or three to another person or entity. A transfer is defined in section 101 of the Copyright Act as an "assignment, mortgage, grant of an exclusive license, transfer by will or intestate succession, or any other change in the ownership of any or all of the exclusive rights in a copyright whether or not it is limited in time or place of effect."

Generally, there are three types of transfers: (1) a nonexclusive license (you remain the owner of your work, and the licensee can use your work but cannot exclude others from doing so); (2) an exclusive license (you remain the owner of your work but no one other than the licensee can use the work – not even you); and (3) an assignment (you give ownership of your work to the transferee). Further limits on transfer include the number of rights transferred, the term, and the geographical scope. To be valid, the transfer of exclusive rights must be in a written agreement signed by the owner of the rights conveyed (or the owner's authorized agent). But nonexclusive transfer of a right does not require a written agreement. So for example, the transfer of the exclusive right of publication to a publisher or agent requires a signed agreement, but the transfer of the nonexclusive right to reproduce an excerpt of a literary work in a newsletter does not.

As a matter of course, however, you should get all agreements relating to your copyright interests in writing. Having a signed agreement memorializes the terms and reduces the likelihood of misunderstandings as to what was promised by each party. (See chapter 12 for more information about contracts.)

A copyright may also be transferred by operation of law. For instance, copyright can be bequeathed by will or by state law if an individual dies without a will. Copyright is a personal property right, and it is subject to the various state laws and regulations that govern the ownership, inheritance, or transfer of personal property and the terms of contracts or conduct of business. For information about relevant state laws, consult an attorney in your area.

Copyright assignments can be filed (or recorded) in the Copyright Office as transfers of copyright ownership. Recording the assignment gives notice to the world that the copyright interest has been transferred. Although you are not required to record the transfer to make it valid, recording the assignment does provide certain legal advantages and may be required to validate the transfer against third parties. For instance, under certain conditions, recordation establishes the order of priority between conflicting transfers (that is, who received the transfer first), or between a conflicting transfer and a nonexclusive license. Recordation also establishes a public record of the transaction and provides "constructive notice," which is a legal term meaning that members of the public are deemed to have been notified even if they have not actually received notice of the transfer. To establish constructive notice, the recorded document must describe the work with specificity so that it could be identified by a reasonable search, and the work must be registered with the Copyright Office.

Reclaiming Your Copyright after Transfer

Did you know that regardless of the terms of your transfer document (e.g., a publishing agreement or a license), you have the right to reclaim your copyright? Discussion about this little-known legal right for authors is all but nonexistent in the publishing industry, and for obvious reasons. Publishers, for instance, may not want authors to know that the "life of copyright" term in most publishing agreements can be rendered null and void if a statutory termination is properly effected. But because different versions of the copyright law apply to different works, depending on when they were created, registered, and transferred, and depending on who transferred the rights, there are different rules for terminating transfers of those works to third parties. I will examine pre-1978 transfers and those transfers made on or after January 1, 1978; but if you have a specific question regarding a potential transfer termination, please contact an intellectual property attorney who is well versed in literary law and transfer termination issues.

Pre-1978 Transfers:

Due to several amendments to copyright law, pre-1978 works, governed by the Copyright Act of 1909, can be protected for up to ninety-five years. This includes the initial twenty-eight-year term of copyright (the initial term), plus the first twenty-eight-year renewal term (renewal term), plus an additional nineteen-year term (bonus term), and, thanks to Sonny Bono, the extended twenty-year term (extended bonus term). Through this series of statutory revisions, pre-1978 authors enjoy an additional sixty-seven years beyond the initial term of protection (provided the renewal was either affirmatively or automatically renewed).

But transfer rules do not hinge on the date of creation or registration per se but on the date the copyright was transferred. Section 304(c) of the Copyright Act allows a writer to reclaim his or her copyright if those rights were transferred (either by the writer or his or her heirs) before January 1, 1978. The window of opportunity to begin the transfer termination process begins either fifty-six years after the date the copyright was originally secured or on January 1, 1978, whichever is later. For pre-1978 transfers, writers actually have two opportunities to reclaim copyright; if the first opportunity fifty-six years after transfer passes, the second and final opportunity to recapture the last twenty years of copyright protection occurs seventy-five years after transfer. You must give at least two years but not more than ten years notice to the transferee that you intend to terminate the copyright transfer.

Post-1977 Transfers:

Creators of works transferred on or after January 1, 1978, enjoy similar but not identical transfer termination rules. Section 203 of the Copyright Act provides that a transfer or license of copyright (or any right in the bundle of rights) executed by the author (but unlike a pre-1978 transfer not a transfer made by anyone other than the author) on or after January 1, 1978, is subject to termination under the following conditions:

☑ A single author who executed a grant may terminate it. If the author is deceased, then whoever is entitled to exercise more than one-half of that author's rights may terminate it.

☑ If two or more authors executed a grant of a joint work, a majority of the authors who executed it may terminate it. If any of the joint authors is dead, his or her termination interest may be exercised by whoever is entitled to exercise more than one-half of that author's interest.

This single, extremely valuable section of the Copyright Act, allowing for the reclaiming of rights by terminating transfers, empowers authors.

Note that the statutory termination provision does not apply to works made for hire or to transfers made by will. The termination right also does not apply to rights arising under foreign laws or derivative works. In the case of derivative works (for example, a movie based on a book), termination of the rights to the underlying work (the book) does not prevent the continued display and distribution of the derivative movie. Once the rights are terminated, however, no new derivative works can be created.

Not surprisingly, the rules to exercise the statutory termination right are specific and must be strictly adhered to or the right will be forever lost.

First, termination can be effected only during a five-year window of opportunity. For works transferred on or after January 1, 1978, the window begins thirty-five years after the grant was made. Special rules apply if the right transferred is the right of publication. In that case, the window begins thirty-five years from the date of publication or at the end of forty years from the date the transfer was executed, whichever is earlier. Presumably, this modification accounts for the gap in time between the date a publishing agreement is signed and the date the work is actually published.

Second, the original owner must deliver to the grantee a signed, written, advance termination notice, which includes the effective date of termination, not less than two years or more than ten years before the termination is to take effect. The notice must be in writing, declare the effective date of termination, and be signed by the original owner (or owners, as per the statute) or a duly authorized agent, who may be an attorney-in-fact under a power of attorney, or, if the original owner is deceased, an heir or beneficiary under a will. The notice must be recorded with the Copyright Office before the termination is to take place, and, of course, the underlying work must be registered with the Copyright Office.

Third, the Copyright Act states, "Termination of the grant may be effected notwithstanding any agreement to the contrary ..." Therefore, you cannot "contract around" this right. In other words, you cannot waive these rights by contract. Your right to terminate exists until it is exercised or lost, pursuant to the terms of the statute.

> Let's bring this topic home by way of example. Assume that Author, at age 30, signs a publishing agreement with XYZ Publisher on January 1, 2003. In that agreement, Author transfers to XYZ the right to publish in hardback and paperback and all subsidiary rights (see chapter 13). The work is published eighteen months later, on July 1, 2004. On January 1, 2010, XYZ licenses the right to develop a motion picture based on the book.
>
> Because the transferring contract was signed on January 1, 2003, before the publication date, the five-year window springs into effect thirty-five years later, on January 1, 2038, and ends on January 1, 2043. During that window, Author has the right to terminate the agreement and reclaim all rights transferred to Publisher. If Author intends to terminate the publishing agreement on the first date the window comes into effect, she will have to send a termination notice to the Publisher or his assignee no earlier than January 1, 2028, and no later than January 1, 2036. Once the transfer terminates, Publisher can no longer create any derivative works or license that right to others.

It is crucial to understand when the termination window exists and to plan properly to reclaim your rights. Additionally, you should plan for the reclamation of your rights in your will so that your family, executor, or trustee knows that your intellectual property exists and understands how to manage and protect those rights after your death. This, of course, means that you must consult a trust and estates attorney familiar with intellectual property laws to create an estate plan that includes a will and perhaps a trust, financial power of attorney, and healthcare power of attorney with a medical directive (aka a living will), so that you protect not only your personal property and real estate but also your intellectual property. In particular, consider creating a testamentary trust in your will to name a literary trustee knowledgeable about intellectual property to maintain and administer your intellectual property rights after your death. This is a special type of trustee who will probably be someone other than a person you would usually name because the literary trustee should be familiar with intellectual property law.

37

Copyright Office Contact Information

☑ Mailing address:

> Library of Congress
> Copyright Office
> Reference & Bibliography Section LM-451
> 101 Independence Avenue SE
> Washington DC 20559-6000

☑ Internet address: www.copyright.gov

☑ Public Information Office (live and recorded information): 202-707-3000 (8:30 a.m. to 5 p.m. Eastern time), Monday through Friday, except federal holidays

☑ Forms and Publications Hotline: 202-707-9100 (24 hours a day, 7 days a week). Request application forms and informational circulars by name or number. If you are unsure which form or circular to order, call the Public Information Office instead.

☑ Fax-on-Demand: 202-707-2600 (24 hours a day, 7 days a week). Use only to request informational circulars. Application forms are not available by fax but can be downloaded at the Web site.

☑ TTY: 202-707-6737. For the hearing impaired. Messages may be left on the TTY line 24 hours a day. Calls are returned between 8:30 a.m. and 5 p.m., Eastern time, Monday through Friday, except federal holidays.

Copyright Registration
of Online Works
Chapter 3

The question often arises as to how the Copyright Act applies to online works. The Internet and other technological advances certainly do present numerous challenges to existing copyright law. But an online work is no different from its physical counterpart, except for the way the information is viewed or perceived. Therefore, there is no one form used specifically to register online works. In fact, the Copyright Office advises that the forms TX, PA, VA, and SR are mainly for office administrative purposes and therefore, technically, a work may be registered on any form.

Of course you should try to use the form most appropriate for your particular situation, and this decision depends on the nature of the online work you want to register. Here are some guidelines to help you choose the proper form:

☑ Form TX 📄 – if text predominates, and there are few or
   no images or sounds appearing in the work

☑ Form VA 📄 – if pictures or graphics predominate the work,
   even if there are accompanying words

☑ Form PA 📄 – if audiovisual material (sound connected to
   images, like an online video) predominates

☑ Form SR 📄 – if sounds predominate (except the sounds
   that accompany and are intrinsic to an audiovisual work)

Also consider that some Web sites can be considered serials (recurring regularly, like a weekly e-newsletter or e-bulletin). In that case, the following forms should be considered:

☑ Form SE 📄 – for a single issue of a serial

☑ Form SE/GROUP 📄 – for a group of issues of a serial,
   including daily newsletters

☑ Form GR/CP 📄 – for a group of contributions to a periodical,
   and used in conjunction with Form TX, PA, or VA

Your registration form should refer only to copyrightable information that is clearly identified in the form, has not been previously registered or published, and is not in the public domain. For published online works, the registration form should include only the content of the work actually published on the date given on the application.

Revisions and Updates

Problems of registration arise when a Web site is updated frequently. The question arises as to whether it is necessary to register the site after each update. For individual works the answer, technically, is yes because there is no comprehensive registration to cover revisions published on different dates. Therefore, each daily update would have to be registered separately. As an attorney, I recommend that you do register each update to be fully protected. I recognize, however, that this would require much work, and I acknowledge that most people don't follow this practice because they find it to be impractical. If you are like most people, then I suggest that you make it a practice to register your Web site every three months. If you do that, then you will be entitled to statutory damages and attorney fees if you ever have to sue someone for infringement. A different rule governs automated databases and serials because they qualify to use blanket registration (see below).

Automated Databases

Some frequently updated online works, like Amazon.com®, are considered automated databases, because the Web sites consist of facts, data, and other pre-existing information organized in files for retrieval by means of a computer. When that is so, a group of updates to the database, whether published or unpublished, that cover up to three months within the same calendar year may be combined in a single, blanket registration. For more information about online databases, review Copyright Office Circular 65.

E-Newsletters and Other E-Serials

40 Group registration is defined by the Copyright Office as a single registration covering multiple issues published on different dates. Group registration is available for works published weekly or less often (serials) and for newsletters published daily or more often than weekly, including those published online. The requirements vary, depending on the type of work. See Copyright Office Circular 62 for more information on serials. Note that group registration is available only for collective works, such as a collection of articles or an anthology, and not for electronic journals published one article at a time.

What Samples of Online Works to Send to the Copyright Office

For online works, the Copyright Office requires a deposit of one of the following:

Option A: A computer disk, labeled with the name of the title and author, that contains the entire work and a representative portion of the work in a format such as a printout, audiocassette, or videotape that can be reviewed by the Copyright Office. If the work is five pages or fewer of text or artwork, or three minutes or fewer of music, sounds, or audiovisual material, send the entire work as the deposit and note that it is complete. If the work is longer than that, deposit five representative pages or three representative minutes.

Option B: A reproduction of the entire work, regardless of length, in the format appropriate for the work being registered. For example, send a printout of a Web site made up of text or images, an audiocassette of sounds, or a videotape of audiovisual material. With this option, no computer disk is required.

These options apply when the work appears online only. If a work is published both online (for example, at the creator's Web site) and by the distribution of physical copies (an author's book, an artist's poster) in any format, then you must follow the regulations for depositing the copies.

For computer programs, databases, and works fixed in CD-ROM format transmitted online, the Copyright Office provides some guidance in Circulars 61 and 65. The office defines a computer program as "a set of statements or instructions to be used directly or indirectly in a computer in order to bring about a certain result." Deposit requirements for computer programs vary according to whether or not the work contains trade secrets. Trade secrets are defined by legal treatises as "any information that can be used in the operation of a business or other enterprise and that is sufficiently valuable and secret to afford an actual or potential economic advantage over others." If your work contains trade secrets, then you should include a cover letter stating that it does, along with the page containing the copyright notice, if any, and one of the following:

For entirely new computer programs

☑ The first and last twenty-five pages of source code with portions containing trade secrets blocked out

☑ The first and last ten pages of source code alone, with no blocked-out portions

☑ The first and last twenty-five pages of object code plus any ten or more consecutive pages of source code, with no blocked-out portions

☑ For programs fifty pages or fewer in length, the entire source code with trade secret portions blocked out

For revised computer programs

☑ If revisions are present in the first and last twenty-five pages, any one of the four options above, as appropriate

☑ If revisions are not present in the first and last twenty-five pages, twenty pages of source code containing the revisions with no blocked-out portions, or any fifty pages of source code containing the revisions with some portions blocked out

For automated databases

☑ For a single-file database (which contains data records pertaining to a single common subject matter), the first and last twenty-five pages or, under a grant of special relief if you do not want to disclose trade secrets, the first and last twenty-five data records

☑ For multiple-file databases (which contain separate and distinct groups of data records), the first fifty data records from each file, or the entire file, whichever is smaller; or fifty pages of data records total under a grant of special relief. Also, you must include a descriptive statement that includes the title of the database; the name and address of copyright claimant; and the name and content of each separate file within the database, including subject matter, origin of data, and number of separate records within each file. For published multiple-file databases, also include a description and sample of the exact contents of any copyright notice used in or with the database (plus manner and frequency of display).

☑ For a revised database (either single or multiple file), fifty pages or records showing the revisions, or the entire revised portions if fewer than fifty pages

For works fixed in CD-ROM format, deposit one complete copy of the CD-ROM, including any operating software or instruction manual, if applicable.

Other People's Words:
Fair Use, Permissions, and
Work Made for Hire
Chapter 4

Writers frequently want to quote from works written by others. Writers and publishers engage the services of editors, indexers, and others who may change or add words in the process of helping to create a finished work. What does the Copyright Act say in regard to such use of words written by others?

???? Songs can be quoted without permission.

The popular belief about quoting songs is incorrect. In most cases you must get a print license from the copyright owner if you quote song lyrics in your book or article, even if the quote is included in a textbook. Getting permission is relatively simple and can be obtained with an adaptation of the short permissions form like the one on page 185 in Appendix B and on the CD-ROM that accompanies this book.

Fair Use

The doctrine of fair use significantly limits copyright protection. This doctrine permits use of copyrighted materials for certain purposes listed in the Copyright Act, such as criticism, comment, news reporting, teaching (including multiple copies for classroom use), scholarship, or research. While technically infringing on the copyright owner's rights, these uses are considered permissible; and such fair use can be used as a defense against a claim of copyright infringement. This concept should not be confused with "public domain" discussed below.

Unfortunately, the proper application of fair use is at best difficult to determine. Contrary to popular belief, there is no specific number of words, lines, or notes of a copyrighted work that may safely be used without permission. Also, it is not sufficient simply to acknowledge the source of the copyrighted material. If your use is not fair use (and if no other exception, such as those explained in chapter 5, applies), you must obtain permission.

???? A certain number of words of copyrighted material can be used without the permission of the owner.

This myth among writers that using, say, 500 words or less of any copyrighted material is always fair use is just that: a myth. It is not true. In fact, copyright law does not set a precise amount of a copyrighted work that can be used without the owner's permission. The Copyright Act provides a series of factors to be considered to determine whether fair use exists.

How to Establish Fair Use

The Copyright Act provides four factors to determine, on a case-by-case basis, whether fair use or infringement exists.

☑ **Character or Purpose of Use:** Allowable use includes criticism (reviews), comment (reviews), news reporting, teaching (classroom), scholarship (reference materials), research (law review articles), and parody (as in the book *The Wind Done Gone*, by Alice Randall). Note that use for commercial purposes will not automatically preclude a finding of fair use. Therefore, compiling a book of movie reviews does not, in itself, defeat a fair use argument.

☑ **Nature of Copyrighted Work:** A court takes into consideration the type of work involved – for example, whether it is fiction or nonfiction, published or unpublished. Jonathan Kirsch, author of *Kirsch's Handbook of Publishing Law*, states that in general a court is less likely to find fair use when a work of fiction or fantasy is copied than when one dealing with facts and figures is copied, or when the work is unpublished or consists of private letters.

☑ **Amount and Substantiality of the Copied Work:** Although no set number of words determines fair use, a court will consider how much of the copyrighted work was used (in other words, did you use one word or a few words, or did you use a large portion of the whole work). Infringement can be found, however, even when only a few words are used if those words are the heart of the copyrighted work.

☑ **Effect on the Potential Market:** A court will ask whether use of the copyrighted work lessens the value of that work. If the use harms the copyright owner's ability to benefit financially from the copyrighted work, it is less likely that fair use exists. If, however, the quoted material is properly credited to the owner and that credit increases the likelihood of sales for the owner, then it is more likely that fair use exists.

Unfortunately, applying these four factors often raises more questions than it answers, and even a comprehensive analysis of the factors provides no absolute conclusions. Only a judge can make the ultimate decision as to whether a particular use is fair.

The Impact of New Technologies on Fair Use Analysis: The fair use doctrine was created in a time when the main mode of transmitting creative works was in print form. With new technologies that allow one person to store large amounts of information in digital form and transmit that same information in perfect condition to millions of people with a few clicks of the mouse, it is easy (and scary) to imagine the innumerable infringements of copyrighted work that exist every second of every day and that remain unpoliced and incapable of control. In light of this twenty-first century reality, some scholars believe that the law lags far behind in closing the gap between yesterday's statutes and today's technology.

Public Domain

The concept of fair use should not be confused with the concept of public domain. With fair use, copyright protection exists and a copyright infringement occurs, but fair use is a legal defense to infringement that "excuses" the violation. On the contrary, when a work is in the public domain it has no copyright protection, and anyone can freely use the work. Therefore, the public – rather than a particular individual or entity – owns the work.

A work might be in the public domain for one of four reasons: (1) the term or copyright protection has expired; (2) the author failed to fulfill a requirement (known as a formality) and therefore lost the right to receive copyright protection; (3) the work was created by the U.S. government or for some other reason is not protected by copyright law; or (4) the copyright owner actually dedicated the work to the public domain. As a rule of thumb, registered works created before 1925 are now in the public domain.

Getting Permission to Use the Work of Others 📄

To acquire permission from a copyright owner to use his or her copyrighted work in, for instance, your manuscript, you must use a permissions request. Perhaps you want to include a quotation or excerpt from another author's copyrighted work, or a photograph or an illustration, and your use would not be considered fair use (and we have already discussed how difficult it is to determine whether fair use exists). In that case, or even if fair use clearly exists, you should consider getting permission in writing. Also, when you sign a publishing agreement, you will often be required to obtain any necessary written permissions to use copyrighted material because the publisher does not want to be exposed to legal liability for infringement.

A permissions request should

☑ describe the copyrighted material with great specificity

☑ note the source of the material

☑ state whether the material has been previously published and, if so, state the date, author, publisher, and current owner

☑ include a grant of permission that specifically states how the material can be used, including any limitations on use (if applicable)

☑ state whether the grant is exclusive or nonexclusive (and if nonexclusive, whether it is revocable or irrevocable)

☑ include specifications for copyright notice and credit

45

☑ include a declaration of control in which the owner expressly states that he or she is the sole owner and has the power to give the requested permission, or if not the sole owner, whom you should contact to get the necessary signatures from the other owners. As a matter of efficiency, you should try to get all owners to sign off on the same permissions form.

Finding out how to reach the person who has the authority to grant permission to use pictures, quotes, and other copyrighted work can be difficult. Here are some possibilities:

☑ Copyright and permissions request information is listed on the back of the title page in most books.

☑ The Copyright Clearance Center, Inc. (CCC) – www.copyright.com (not to be confused with the unrelated Copyright Office at www.copyright.gov.) – is a licensor of text reproduction rights. Contact CCC to get permission to reproduce copyrighted content such as articles and book chapters in your journals, photocopies, course packs, library reserves, Web sites, and e-mail.

☑ National Writers Union (NWU) represents freelance writers in American markets. For permissions to use articles by freelance writers, contact NWU via the Publication Rights Clearinghouse: prc@nwu.org.

☑ Harry Fox Agency (HFA – National Music Publisher's Association) is the leading mechanical licensing, collections, and distribution agency for U.S. music publishers. Contact HFA at http://www.harryfox.com or 711 Third Avenue, New York, NY 10017, Tel: (212) 370-5330, Fax: (646) 487-6779.

☑ ASCAP (American Society of Composers, Authors and Publishers) is a performing rights organization that licenses the rights of its member songwriters, composers, and publishers at www.ascap.com. It is a licensor of public performance rights and can be reached as follows:
- Internet licensing: weblicense@ascap.com
- Cable or satellite licensing: cablelicensing@ascap.com
- Television licensing: TVLicensing@ascap.com
- Radio licensing: radiolicensing@ascap.com
- General licensing: licensing@ascap.com

☑ BMI (Broadcast Music, Inc.) is a performing rights organization that licenses the public performance rights of its member songwriters, composers, and publishers at www.bmi.com or 320 West 57th Street, New York, NY 10019-3790, (212) 586-2000.

☑ SESAC (Society of European Stage Authors and Composers) is a performing rights organization that licenses the public performance rights of its member songwriters, composers, and publishers at www.sesac.com.

☑ Icopyright.com is an online licensor of digital content (work published on the Internet) at www.icopyright.com.

☑ The Photographer's Index connects the public with owners of photographic works at www.photographersindex.com.

Work Made for Hire

As you know by now, a copyright generally exists in a work as soon as it is created in a fixed and tangible form. The creator of the work owns and controls the bundle of rights associated with copyright. An exception to that rule is the work-made-for-hire doctrine, in which the creator is not the owner for purposes of copyright protection. The Copyright Act provides strict guidelines that determine whether a work-made-for-hire situation exists.

Work made for hire can occur in two contexts: that involving employers and employees and that involving independent contractors. In the first, work made for hire is done by employees within the scope of their employment. In the second, an independent contractor is specially commissioned to perform work for one of the following purposes only:

- ☑ a contribution to a collective work
- ☑ a part of a motion picture or other audiovisual work
- ☑ a translation
- ☑ a supplementary work, which includes such things as forewords, editorial changes, and indexes
- ☑ a compilation
- ☑ an instructional text
- ☑ a test
- ☑ answer material for a test
- ☑ a sound recording
- ☑ an atlas

Furthermore, the work performed by the independent contractor is considered to be work made for hire only if the contractor and the hiring person both sign a contract before the work begins, stating that the work is made for hire.

Because the existence of work made for hire depends on the relationship of the parties involved, the first question to answer is whether the creator is an employee or an independent contractor.

Employee: In the employer/employee relationship, the employer controls the work product, work site, work schedule, and assignments; provides the equipment used to perform the work; pays the employee a regular salary and takes appropriate deductions; and so forth. For example, a staff writer is an employee of a newspaper company. In that situation, the newspaper company and not the staff writer owns the copyright of all work produced by the writer during his or her employment.

Independent contractor: Unlike employees, independent contractors maintain control over how the work they do is done. Independent contractors are in business for themselves. They provide their own equipment, and set their own hours and work schedule. They may refer to themselves as business owners, freelancers, self-employed, or consultants. They are their own bosses.

If you want an independent contractor to contribute to your product, and you want to retain copyright to his or her contribution, then as stated earlier you must both sign a work-made-for-hire agreement before the work begins. You will find a sample agreement in Appendix B, but here's a checklist of important items that should be included in any work-made-for-hire agreement:

☑ the name, type of entity (corp., LLC, etc.), and address of each party

☑ a paragraph that sets forth the complete description of the work and the amount of compensation involved

☑ a list of all rights included, which should be the entire bundle of rights

☑ a statement that the creator has no rights in the work created or in the work in which the creation is used

☑ an assignment provision that assigns all rights, in case the work-made-for-hire agreement fails for any reason

☑ representations and warranties

☑ a confidentiality provision

☑ a clause that addresses what happens if the work is not completed or if you stop work before it's completed

☑ due dates

☑ a clause dealing with information you give to the independent contractor in order to create the work and all work product, which should remain your property

☑ signature lines for all parties

When Someone Violates
Your Copyright
Chapter 5

Copyright infringement is the violation of any of the rights in the bundle of rights explained in chapter 2 — that is, the rights of reproduction, adaptation, distribution, public performance, and public display; the rights of attribution and integrity (see chapter 10); and the right of importation. The Digital Millennium Copyright Act (DMCA), described in chapter 10, extended the existing Copyright Act to specifically address works on the Internet.

The Limits of Copyright Protection

Although it is illegal for anyone to violate any of a copyright owner's rights, these rights are not unlimited in scope, and the Copyright Act establishes certain limitations on these rights.

What You Can Do with a Copy of Copyrighted Work: The owner of a particular copy of copyrighted work — a book, for instance — that was lawfully obtained may sell or otherwise dispose of that particular copy without the authority of the copyright owner. So if you buy a book, magazine, or CD, for example, you can give it away, sell it, or even throw it away without the copyright owner's consent.

> The right of owners of copies of a copyrighted work to dispose of those copies can have interesting implications for self-published authors. For instance, at Amazon.com® each product page lists the copies sold by Amazon.com®, and Amazon.com® offers third parties the opportunity to sell their copies of the author's work from the same page through the Amazon Marketplace Sellers Program. Copies sold by Marketplace Sellers are in direct competition with the copies listed by Amazon.com®, usually at a discount. This means that self-published authors who use the Amazon.com® Advantage program to distribute their books may lose sales to third parties, who often undercut the listed price. According to the Copyright Act, however, these third parties are within their rights to dispose of their copies without the copyright owner's consent. (Note that this right does not apply to computer software in most cases).

Reproduction Rights for Libraries and Archives: The Copyright Act expressly permits libraries and archives to reproduce and distribute copyrighted work provided that (1) the purpose of reproduction and distribution is not for direct or indirect financial gain; and (2) the collections are available to the public or, in the case of archives, to researchers other than those already affiliated with the archive. This exception to the rights granted to copyright owners relates mostly to literary works as opposed to sound, pictorial, sculptural, or audiovisual works. But the Copyright Act limits this right to "no more than one copy . . . of the work."

Performances and Displays in Educational Settings: Teachers and other instructors are exempted from the performance and display restrictions in the Copyright Act. The use must be in face-to-face teaching activities for a nonprofit educational institution, or a regular part of systematic instructional activities of a governmental body or educational institution, and must be directly related and of material assistance to the teaching process and educational content. The recipients must be students, disabled people, or government employees.

Reproduction for the Blind and Those with Other Disabilities: This exemption allows reproduction and distribution of copies of copyrighted works in particular formats suited for the blind and people with other disabilities.

Ideas, Methods, Systems: Only the actual (tangible) expression of the author can be protected by copyright. The ideas, plans, methods, or systems described or embodied in a work are not protected by copyright.

Inventions: The Copyright Act does not protect an invention or an inventive design.

Blank Forms and Similar Works: To be copyrightable, a work must possess a baseline amount of literary, pictorial, or musical creative expression. By its very nature, a blank form is created to record and organize rather than to creatively express information. Therefore, a form does not meet the basic creativity threshold required to render it copyrightable.

Works Containing Common Property: Copyright protection does not cover works that consist entirely of information that is common property and that is not original, such as

- ☑ standard calendars
- ☑ height and weight charts
- ☑ tape measures and rulers
- ☑ schedules of sporting events
- ☑ lists or tables taken from public documents or other common sources

50

Works Containing Both Copyrightable and Noncopyrightable Elements: So what do you do when you publish a form, calendar, or schedule not entitled to copyright protection, but it also contains original text, artwork, or some other work that is copyrightable? In this case, copyright protection extends to the copyrightable elements, namely the literary or pictorial work for which copyright protection would otherwise apply, but not to the blank form or other unprotectable aspects of the work.

Names, Pen Names, Book Titles, and Slogans

The Copyright Act does not apply to names, pen names, book titles, or slogans no matter how creative or original they may be. Therefore individual book titles; names of products, services, businesses, organizations, groups, or individual performers; advertising slogans; pen names or stage names; or the mere listing of ingredients cannot be copyrighted. Under certain circumstances, however, brand names, trade names, slogans, phrases, group names, and names of individuals can be protected under the laws of unfair competition, and can be protected and registered under trademark law.

An author can use a pen name (pseudonym) to create a literary work. Note that nicknames or other shortened forms of an author's real name are not considered to be pen names. As stated above, the pen name itself is not subject to copyright protection. If you use a pen name, take care when filling out the registration form in order to avoid supplying confusing information to the Copyright Office. In space 2 of the form, you can use your real name or your pen name (Jolly Roger, pseudonym) or you can leave it blank. Space 4, however, requires the copyright claimant's name and should not be left blank if you are registering under a pseudonym. Note: there is no legal requirement that the author be identified by his or her real name on the application form. If you register your work under a pseudonym, consult an attorney about potential issues involved in proof of ownership.

 Each limitation on copyright protection has precise statutory requirements. For more information about those and other limitations and requirements, see the Copyright Act.

Determining Who Sues and Who Gets Sued

Generally speaking, the legal and beneficial owners of an exclusive right of copyright – which means the author, assignee, or exclusive licensee – have the right to sue for infringement, as long as the copyright is registered with the Copyright Office before initiating a law suit. But the holder of a nonexclusive right, such as a nonexclusive licensee, does not have the right to initiate an infringement suit. Limited exceptions apply in certain instances as, for example, when an individual assigns his or her copyright but retains the right to receive royalties.

Now that you know who can sue, you need to know who can be sued. There are four types of infringers.

Type of Infringer	Description
Direct Infringer	One who actually uses copyrighted material without the consent of the copyright owner.
Contributory Infringer	One who substantially participates in the direct infringement of a copyright interest.
Vicarious Infringer	One who has the right and ability to supervise the actions of a direct infringer and has a financial stake in the infringing activity.
Criminal Infringer	One who infringes a copyright willfully either for the purpose of "commercial advantage or private financial gain," or by the reproduction or distribution of $1,000 worth of copies of copyrighted work during any 180-day period. A copyright owner must establish more than reproduction and distribution. She or he must also establish willful intent. And, in the case of felony infringement, the owner must establish that a copyright exists, that it was infringed by the defendant by reproduction and distribution of the copyrighted work, and that the defendant acted willfully, and copied or distributed at least ten copies at a value of more than $2,500 within a 180-day period.

Copyright Infringement Remedies

The Copyright Act provides four remedies for copyright infringement. Statutory damages are not available, however, if the infringement began before the work was registered, unless such registration is made *within three months after the first publication of the work.*

52

Injunctions: An injunction is a court declaration to stop the behavior giving rise to the lawsuit. For instance, a court may order an alleged infringer to stop making copies or to stop distributing the copyrighted work. Any court can, in its discretion, grant temporary and final injunctions "on such terms as it may deem reasonable to prevent or restrain infringement of a copyright."

Impounding Infringing Copies: When an infringement case is pending, the court has the discretion to impound all copies or phonorecords claimed to have been made or used in violation of the copyright owner's exclusive rights, and all plates, molds, matrices, masters, tapes, film negatives, or other articles by means of which such copies or phonorecords may be reproduced. If the plaintiff – the one who sues – in an infringement suit wins the case, the court can order the destruction of the copies and the methods of reproduction and distribution.

Damages and Profits: A plaintiff who wins an infringement lawsuit is entitled to either statutory damages or to actual damages and any additional profits of the infringer. If the work was registered within three months of publication, then statutory damages would be available; if not, then only actual damages would be available in addition to profits. To establish the infringer's profits, the copyright owner must present proof only of the infringer's gross revenue, and the infringer must prove his or her deductible expenses and the elements of profit attributable to factors other than the copyrighted work. If statutory damages are available, the plaintiff can recover for all infringements with respect to one work, an amount from $750 to $30,000, in the court's discretion.

In the case of willful infringement, the court has discretion to increase the damage award to a maximum of $150,000. If, however, the defendant establishes innocent infringement, the court can reduce the award to a minimum of $200.

> Statutory damages are awarded for each infringed work, not for each incidence of infringement. For example, if someone infringes the copyrighted work *When Pigs Fly* by making one hundred illegal copies, the copyright owner can recover between $200 and $150,000, not one hundred times that amount.

Costs and Attorney Fees: The court also has the discretion to award court costs and reasonable attorney fees to the prevailing party. The court considers a number of factors, namely, the losing party's frivolousness, motivation, and objective reasonableness, and the court's need to "advance considerations of compensation and deterrents."

Limitations on Actions

Criminal infringement cases must be filed within five years of the time the infringement took place, or the case is barred. Civil infringement actions must be filed within three years after the infringement occurred, or the right to sue is forfeited. These periods of time are commonly referred to as the statute of limitations because the law limits the amount of time during which you can sue.

53

Notable Copyright Infringement Cases

Silverstein v. Penguin Putnam, Inc. — May 4, 2004

Stuart Silverstein published *Not Much Fun: The Lost Poems of Dorothy Parker*, a collection of poems (arranged by subject) by the accomplished poet, writer, and critic, that had not been included in the three books Parker wrote during her lifetime. Silverstein gathered these uncollected poems primarily from magazines and newspapers. In 1994, Silverstein offered Penguin Putnam (Penguin) the opportunity to publish his collection, but Penguin passed. But five years later, Penguin published a similar collection, *Dorothy Parker: Complete Poems*, which included poems from Parker's three books and a new section titled "Poems Uncollected by Parker" that included all but one of the poems in Silverstein's collection and several poems not included in Silverstein's version. All of these poems were ordered chronologically.

Silverstein filed a lawsuit against Penguin, arguing that he had a copyright in the selection, copyediting, and arrangement of the Parker poems. Interestingly, the actual copyright owner of all Parker poems was not involved in the lawsuit. A New York district court found in Silverstein's favor and ordered Penguin not to sell or distribute any more copies of *Complete Poems*. On appeal, however, the Second Circuit court reversed the lower court order and challenged Silverstein's case because of the lack of creativity – a key component of copyright – exhibited in his collection. Without creativity (and the second element of originality), no protectable interest exists. Cases have held that a compiler of previously published work can have a copyright in a collection if there is some minimal level of creativity in the selection process. Therefore, on May 7, 2004, the Second Circuit sent the case back to the lower court for a rehearing in light of these findings and to determine whether Silverstein is entitled to money damages. The Second Circuit also found that it was improper to prevent Penguin from selling and distributing its collection.

At the time of publication, this case was still awaiting the new District Court decision.

The Tarzan Case – August 29, 2003

This case deals with the 1909 version of the Copyright Act and the work-made-for-hire doctrine. Edgar Rice Burroughs published *Tarzan of the Apes* in 1912 and *Jungle Tales of Tarzan* in 1916–17, and both are now in the public domain. Burroughs created ERB in 1923 to manage his literary rights. In 1937, United Features Syndicate hired Burne Hogarth to illustrate the comic strip *Tarzan*, which he did until 1950. In the 1960s, Hogarth and Robert Hodes, the vice president of ERB, discussed a new version of Tarzan books for the adult audience; and in 1971, Hogarth signed an agreement with ERB in which ERB commissioned Hogarth's illustration services and which named ERB as the copyright holder of the book in its entirety. In exchange, ERB paid Hogarth $5,000 and promised him 50 percent of the proceeds realized by ERB for the book. ERB as sole owner of the copyright entered into a publishing agreement with Watson-Guptill. Watson-Guptill published the book in 1972 and 1976; neither publication earned much money. The publisher filed the copyright registrations but erroneously listed Hogarth as the copyright owner. This error was cured in subsequent filings. Hogarth died in 1996.

On April 1, 1994, ERB licensed the Tarzan character to Disney and received $15 million in licensing revenue. After Disney released a Tarzan movie in 1999, Hogarth's estate sent a cease-

and-desist letter to Disney and ERB, and ultimately filed this lawsuit to reap some financial benefit from the success of the Tarzan character and story.

However, the district court found, and the appeals court affirmed, that Hogarth was not the author, as defined in the Copyright Act, but a commissioned illustrator who created illustrations on a work-made-for-hire basis. Accordingly, he had no copyright ownership rights.

The AOL Case — February 10, 2004

In *Ellison v. AOL* 2004, Harlan Ellison, a short-story writer, filed contributory and vicarious copyright liability claims (see page 52 for more information about the various types of copyright infringement) against AOL because an AOL user, Stephen Robertson, posted Ellison's short stories on a peer-to-peer file sharing network to which AOL provided Internet access. AOL attempted to sidestep liability by asserting safe harbor limitations of liability under the Digital Millennium Copyright Act (DMCA). The DMCA limits the liability of Internet service providers (ISPs) under certain circumstances (see page 89 for more information about that act). In this case, AOL maintained the posted peer-to-peer information for fourteen days before purging it from the server. The district court held that AOL was not guilty of vicarious infringement (which requires financial benefit and the ability to control the infringing activity), that there may be contributory infringement, and that nonetheless AOL qualified for safe harbor. On appeal, the Sixth Circuit court declared that because infringing materials stayed on AOL's servers for fourteen days, AOL might not qualify for safe harbor, and sent the case back to the district court to continue the trial for that issue only. It is not clear at this point whether ISPs will be able to slip through this liability loophole.

(this page is intentionally blank—this type does NOT print)

Other Legal Issues to Consider
Chapter 6

The First Amendment states that "Congress shall make no law . . . abridging the freedom of speech, or of the press." One of the core components of the First Amendment is the freedom of speech, which protects individual expression from interference or control by the government. The Supreme Court requires a substantial justification before it will permit violation of this right. But some speech that would breach the peace or might cause violence has been prohibited. Perhaps the best-known example is the prohibition against yelling "fire" in a crowded theater.

Some scholars and critics suggest that the First Amendment conflicts with an author's right under the Copyright Act (based on article I, section 8 of the Constitution) to hold exclusive rights to his or her creations. At least in theory, however, both sections of the Constitution work together to balance the rights of the individual with the rights of society as a whole. For example, the First Amendment allows the free exchange of ideas while the Copyright Act protects the individual's physical manifestation of those ideas.

Still, this balance tips in favor of free speech and society, and against copyright protection, when copyrighted material is so newsworthy that courts may declare it is in the public interest to share certain work without the copyright owner's permission. For instance, in the federal district court case of *Time Inc. v. Bernard Geis Assocs.*, the court permitted public use of copyrighted film footage of the assassination of President John F. Kennedy without the copyright owner's consent.

Using Someone's Name or Likeness in Your Work

Cashing in on one's celebrity is big business these days. Salaries for sports and entertainment figures are certainly impressive. But these million-dollar salaries are often dwarfed when compared to the multimillion-dollar deals based on using a person's name or image to endorse a product or service.

This use of a person's name or likeness for commercial gain involves one of the lesser known intellectual property rights – the right of publicity. The right of publicity is a person's exclusive right to use, and to prevent the unauthorized use of, his or her name, likeness, or other aspect of his or her persona (collectively referred to as persona) for commercial gain. The definition of "persona" goes beyond a person's image and can include words or sounds that are intended to remind the audience of the person, a look-alike, a nickname or phrase commonly associated with the person, and even his or her former name. Therefore, the potential for a right-of-publicity claim exists any time you use someone's persona (or an imitation of it) in your book, article, or other literary or artistic work.

The first case to acknowledge the right of publicity was *Haelan Laboratories Inc. v. Topps Chewing Gum, Inc.* in 1953, in which the court recognized the valuable property right of a baseball player's photograph when used on trading cards. In a prominent right-of-publicity case, *White v. Samsung Electronics America, Inc.* (1993), the court found that an advertisement which featured a set similar to the *Wheel of Fortune* show and a robotic Vanna White look-alike infringed Vanna White's right of publicity. The court found in her favor and extended the right-of-publicity protection to include not only name and likeness but also identity.

In September 2002, Tom Cruise and Nicole Kidman sued Sephora, Inc., a cosmetics company, in a Los Angeles court for allegedly using a picture of them without permission in a brochure to advertise the company's so-called celebrity scents. They sued under several legal theories, including California's common law right of publicity and unfair competition, and under the Lanham Act.

Other notable right-of-publicity lawsuits filed by the rich and famous include a 2003 case of Spike Lee against TNN, its corporate parents MTV and Viacom, and its president, Albie Hecht, for naming its 2003 "first network for me" Spike TV; and the Tiger Woods trademark infringement, trademark dilution, and right-of-publicity suit against Jireh for selling lithographs of Rob Rush's *The Masters of Augusta*, depicting Tiger Woods's win at the Masters in 1997 while previous winners observed him.

There is no federally protected right of publicity. This right is protected in some states by common law developed by cases; in other states it is protected by statute developed by legislative bodies. In fact, some states refer to this right as the right of publicity but others do not; instead, they protect the right under other legal theories such as the right of privacy or unfair competition (defined as appropriating the commercial value of a person's identity by using the person's name, likeness, or other characteristics of identity without consent for purposes of trade). And some states do not protect this right at all. But under a federal law known as the Lanham Act, a person may be able to establish a claim for the unauthorized use of his or her identity if it creates a false endorsement. And, if you have trademarked your name as certain celebs have done – Tiger Woods, Spike Lee, Oprah, Rosie (O'Donnell), Madonna, or Martha (Stewart), just to name a few – you may be able to assert trademark infringement and dilution claims under the Lanham Act.

Also, while most states protect the rights of both celebrities and noncelebrities, a minority of states protect the right of publicity for celebrities only. And some states protect a person's right of publicity only if they have already established value in their persona by commercially exploiting

58

it in the past. Therefore, the rationale for protecting only celebrities seems to be based on the argument that a noncelebrity's persona has no commercial value. But some general guidelines and exceptions have emerged from this piecemeal set of state laws dealing with the right of publicity. In some cases a public figure's heirs have a legal right of publicity in the dead person's name, voice, signature, photograph, or likeness.

The absence of a federal right-of-publicity law and the wide differences in laws from state to state become more and more problematic as technology continues to increase exponentially the ways in which publicity rights can be violated either innocently or with intent. There is talk of a federal law; however, although desperately needed, none exists yet.

Exceptions: The two main exceptions to the right of publicity, the newsworthiness exception and the incidental use exception, are based on the First Amendment's balance between free speech and the right of publicity.

The newsworthiness exception allows a person's name or likeness to be used in a news story without that person's consent as long as the use is considered to be of legitimate public interest or concern. Furthermore, the use cannot mislead the reader into thinking that the person endorses the article, newspaper, book, or whatever vehicle his or her persona appears in. A common way that writers can protect themselves when writing about others is to include a disclaimer making it clear that those others do not endorse the writing.

It is important to note, however, that the newsworthiness exception affords greater protection to some uses and lesser protection to others. For instance, it is more likely to apply in cases of news reporting or information important to or affecting the public, and it may or may not apply to entertainment uses, including fiction. But using someone's persona in an advertising context, to sell a product or service, gets the least protection along this spectrum. The essential point is that an unauthorized use of an individual's persona must have a reasonable relationship to the subject of the report, story, or use.

The exception for incidental use occurs when a person's name is merely mentioned or his or her likeness is used or referred to. If this exception did not exist, the right of publicity could very well stifle creativity. For instance, authors would not be able to authenticate a story line by referring to real people and places. Let's say you're writing a novel that takes place in Los Angeles. Your main character meets a friend for lunch at a deli on Melrose, and they make small talk about a movie star who happens to be sitting in a nearby booth. Can they mention the well-known actor by name? The answer is probably yes, if doing so adds to the artistic authenticity of your work. Such use should be reasonably related to the content of your article, book, or other literary work. The test is whether the use is of interest or concern to the public. This test extends not only to hard news stories but also to sports, entertainment, and similar pieces.

Uses of Someone's Persona: As discussed above, an individual's persona can be used to advertise a product or service. Such use is considered a commercial use. Commercial speech has been defined as doing no more than proposing a commercial transaction (see *Hoffman v. Capital Cities*, 2001). Although commercial speech is entitled to some measure of protection under the First Amendment, it is limited. And where the sole purpose of using the persona in commercial speech is to sell a product or service, no First Amendment protection exists.

Note, however, that it may be permissible to use an individual's persona to help sell a product or service if the use is reasonably related to the content. For instance, *Hoffman v. Capital Cities* resulted because *Los Angeles Magazine* used a photograph of Dustin Hoffman's character image Tootsie as an illustration for the article "Grand Illusions" in the "Fabulous Hollywood" issue. Sixteen other stills from familiar movie scenes were also used in the article that discussed 1997 spring fashions. The caption under the picture in question read, "Dustin Hoffman isn't a drag in a butter-colored silk gown by Richard Tyler and Ralph Lauren heels." The magazine did not obtain permission from Hoffman (the subject) or from the copyright owner (who is generally the photographer who took the picture).

The court found that the use was not pure commercial speech because the picture did not appear in a Ralph Lauren ad or a Richard Tyler ad. Furthermore, in terms of the context of the article, the court found that the use combines fashion photography, humor, and editorial comment on classic films and famous actors.

Use of someone's persona may also be permissible if editorial in nature, that is, if used for news reporting; scholarship; or cultural, historical, educational, political, or public interest reasons. The same consideration is given to artistic use in which an individual's name or likeness appears in a work of fiction that incorporates real people. Again, this use is probably permissible as long as the goal is artistic and of public interest and concern rather than for purely economic gain.

Who Is Entitled to Sue to Protect the Right of Publicity: Most states require a right-of-publicity claimant to be a living person. But a few jurisdictions, most notably California, allow heirs of a deceased person to sue. For the law in your state, contact an attorney familiar with intellectual property and privacy laws in your area.

Defending a Right-of-Publicity Claim: Schuyler M. Moore, Esq., explains in his article "Raising Defenses to Right-of-Publicity Claims" that there is no consistent set of defenses to such claims. The absence of clearly defined laws and defenses presents a major issue for writers who expose themselves to potential right-of-publicity claims with the mere mention of another person's name or likeness in a literary work.

Furthermore, even if you successfully defend your use of a person's name or likeness in your manuscript, you still lose by being sued in the first place and having to defend a costly lawsuit.

Publishing houses hesitate to expose themselves to such liability; to anticipate and avoid it, they subject manuscripts to legal vetting, which means they review manuscripts thoroughly for legal issues. Self-published authors are certainly not immune from legal liability and should submit their manuscripts to the same vetting process. With the potential for professional and personal liability, a self-published author is at greater risk than a large publishing house, which employs an entire legal department devoted exclusively to these issues. Therefore, if you decide to publish your work independently, you should submit your manuscript to a publishing attorney who can vet it, alert you to possible legal issues, and advise you on the best course of action.

Privacy Issues

The American Heritage Dictionary defines the right of privacy as "the quality or condition of being secluded from the presence or view of others." More simply put, it is the right to be left alone. The three generally recognized invasions of privacy include intrusion, unreasonable publicity, and false light.

Intrusion occurs when someone intentionally enters without permission into a place where you have a reasonable expectation of privacy. Intrusion involves issues such as hidden cameras or other surveillance methods, wire tapping, and searching someone's garbage. Therefore, when conducting interviews, you should always inform the subject that you are taping the conversation. To further protect yourself, you should require all interviewees to sign a permissions form authorizing you to tape the conversation and use the content in your literary work. In the case of intrusion claims, a plaintiff is not required to show that the alleged intruder divulged the information obtained to the public. It is sufficient to show that the person entered a place where the plaintiff had a reasonable expectation of privacy (his or her home, for instance).

Unreasonable publicity occurs when intimate or embarrassing facts about a person are divulged to the public (published) in an unfair or irrational way. A court finds such publication to be unreasonable when the information is not of public interest or concern. And it is not enough to argue that the information is true. In fact, privacy laws are intended to protect against the publication of truthful but private information.

False light occurs when a person is portrayed in public in an extremely offensive way. The classic example is when an offensive caption appears beneath someone's picture, a caption that could leave a false and negative impression of the individual in the mind of a reasonable person. A false-light claim can also arise when essential facts are omitted: for example, when a reporter writes that a man was arrested for molesting his seven-year-old son but fails to report that all charges were subsequently dropped when it was discovered the father was out of town during the incident; or when certain elements of a book are fictionalized but it is not clear what is fact and what is fiction, a situation that can be avoided with a clear, well-written disclaimer.

When Discussing Intimate Facts Is OK: Authors are usually permitted to discuss facts that are generally known to the public or are considered newsworthy. But here's a general list of materials that are considered off limits: private letters, e-mail messages, information about sexual proclivities or sexual history, financial or medical information, or other private matters. When discussing the lives of noncelebrities, remember that it is even more difficult to establish that the information is of public concern or interest. The sex life of Madonna, Bill Clinton, or Earvin "Magic" Johnson may be worthy of a tell-all unauthorized biography, but that may not be true of your ex-spouse, unless he or she also happens to be a public figure whose affairs would be considered of public concern or interest.

E-Mail and Privacy

As part of the technology boom of the '80s and '90s, millions of Americans now use e-mail as a quick and inexpensive way to communicate with friends, family, and colleagues both near and far. People assume that e-mail is also secure; however e-mail is far less secure than traditional mail. E-mail, like other types of electronic communication, such as cell phones and pagers, is susceptible to illegal interception. Under the Electronic Communications Privacy Act of 1986 (ECPA), third parties are prohibited from reading private e-mail.

The ECPA extended privacy law to cover new technologies like e-mail, so you must take care to obtain the necessary permissions if you intend to incorporate e-mail messages into your manuscript. Also recognize that e-mail is not a 100-percent-secure communication environment. A good rule of thumb is not to e-mail anything that you would not want sent instantly to millions of people. With one click of the mouse, the recipient could do just that, even though he or she is not supposed to.

Trademark
Chapter 7

Like other business people, Literary Entrepreneurs use trademarks or brands on their products and services to identify them and distinguish them from those of their competitors. The terms *trademark, brand*, and *brand name* are often used interchangeably. A trademark identifies the source of a product or service (which company or individual produces or distributes it), and a brand or brand name is the name given to a certain product or service. Many brands, however, may not be suitable for federal trademark registration yet may clearly identify a certain person, product, or service. For example, Yellow Pages, if used for the business pages of a telephone book, is not suitable for federal trademark because it is generic; yet it is a very strong brand. But The Real Yellow Pages®, The Friendly Yellow Pages®, The Original Yellow Pages®, and 1-800-Yellow Pages® are among the many registered trademarks using the term (brand) Yellow Pages.

Contrary to popular belief, trademarks come into existence the moment you use them to mark your goods or services for your customers. That is worth repeating: trademarks come into existence the moment you use them to mark your goods or services for your customers. You do not have to register your trademark with any governmental agency to bring your trademark into existence. In fact you cannot register your trademark until you have used it with your goods or services. The longer you use your trademark, the stronger it becomes – because it builds goodwill and recognition with your customers. This unregistered use of a trademark is protected under common law. Common law consists of court decisions made by judges and juries rather than of statutes created and passed by legislators. Older cases serve as guidelines (or precedent) to be applied to the facts and circumstances of newer cases.

Trademarks registered under federal and state laws as well as certain unregistered trademarks under common law enjoy exclusive rights. A federally registered trademark will generally give you the right to use the mark in all fifty states and all U.S. territories. A federal trademark also protects consumers by preventing different businesses in the United States from using the same or similar trademarks, which helps to avoid confusion among products and their sources. Protection of trademarks registered under state law is limited to the state of registration; the rules and regulations that affect trademarks vary from state to state. Trademark protections of common law are limited to the geographic area in which the mark has actually been used. The fact that many trademarked products are now marketed and sold via the Internet to a large interstate audience means that a broad common law protection may cover them.

? Is there such a thing as an international trademark?

Answer: No. Although trademarks are available in most foreign countries, registration must be applied for in each of those countries. Under certain international treaties and agreements, including the Madrid Protocol and the Community Trademark in Europe, filing may be made in multiple countries. The Madrid Protocol trademark treaty went into effect in the United States on November 2, 2003. This allows U.S. trademark owners to file for registration in any member country by filing a single standardized application in English, with a single set of fees, through the United States Patent and Trademark Office.

Trademark and Service Mark Defined

A trademark or service mark is one way to identify certain goods or services as those produced or provided by a specific person or company. A service mark is the same as a trademark except that it applies to the source of a service rather than a product. The terms *trademark, mark,* and *brand* are often used interchangeably to refer to both trademarks and service marks, whether they consist of word marks or other types of marks, which will be described below. They may be names, slogans, logos, designs, colors, or other identifying marks. Trademarks date back to about 4000 BC, when different markings were used to identify property belonging to specific owners. Craftsmen reproduced their marks or brands on their products. Farmers branded their livestock, and royal families identified their ancestry with a specific coat of arms.

Over the years this identification method evolved into today's system of trademark registration and protection. This system helps consumers identify and purchase a product or service that meets their needs because its unique trademark indicates its nature and quality. United States law defines trademark as a word, phrase, symbol, or design, or a combination of words, phrases, symbols, or designs that identifies and distinguishes the source of the goods or services of one party from those of others. There are forty-five different classifications of goods and services listed in the "Trademark Acceptable Identification of Goods & Services Manual" online.

64

It used to be the case that if, in the application for federal registration, you entered all the words of your trademark in capital letters and in a standard font, then the registered word or term could be used in any way; but if the words were entered on the application in upper- and lowercase, then the registered mark would be considered only a drawing and protected only for the specific way in which it appeared on the application. Such a distinction no longer exists. Registrants are now able to enter and use the word or term in any way (uppercase, lowercase, sideways, in various colors, in squiggly lines, and so forth).

Trademarks may consist of:

☑ Word mark – one word or a group of words (iPod®, Amistad®, Def Poetry Jam®)

☑ Drawing mark – a black-and-white drawing of words, letters, or numbers in stylized form

☑ Persona – the name or persona of a real person (George Foreman Grills®, Oprah Book Club®, Newman's Own®)

☑ Symbol mark – logo or design (the golden arches of McDonald's, the Nike swoosh)

☑ Three-dimensional mark – the shape and packaging of goods (Coca Cola bottles, yellow-and-black boxes for Kodak Film)

☑ Sound mark – musical, vocal, electronic, or other sound (NBC chimes, AAMCO honk)

☑ Fragrance mark – (smell of plumeria blossoms on embroidery yarn)

☑ Color mark – color schemes or a single color used as a distinguishing feature (pink fiberglass insulation of Corning, colorful plumage of the NBC peacock, brown color associated with UPS vehicles and uniforms)

Normally, a mark for goods appears on the product or on its packaging, label, instruction manual, or container; a service mark appears in advertising and other printed matter related to the services, such as announcements, brochures, publicity releases, invoices, stationery, and business cards. Trademarks indicate to consumers that a particular product comes from a certain source, even if the name of that source is unknown to the consumer. For example, when you go to the grocery store you may buy CHIQUITA® bananas. You most likely don't know the source of the bananas, but you may know that CHIQUITA® brand bananas are consistently tasty and of high quality. Trademarks also create goodwill for their owners by exploiting the established quality and reputation built up over time.

Some examples of registered trademarks and service marks are:

☑ **Essence®** (goods and services) *Owner:* Essence Communications, Inc. A woman's magazine.

☑ **Black Expressions®** ᴮᴸᵃᶜᵏexpreSsions (goods and services) *Owner:* Doubleday Direct, Inc. Mail order book clubs; online retail store services featuring books, prerecorded audio cassettes of music and books readings, prerecorded video cassettes, and gift merchandise.

☑ **Booksense.com** (services) *Owner:* American Bookseller Association. Computerized online ordering services featuring printed books and magazines, prerecorded videos, music, and computer software.

☑ **Oprah®** (services) *Owner:* Harpo, Inc. Entertainment services; a television variety talk show series.

65

☑ Harry Potter® **Harry Potter** (goods) *Owner:* Time Warner Management Company, L.P., American Television and Communications Corporation, and Warner Communications Inc. Books, paper items, ceramics, lithographs; pens, pencils, and cases for them; erasers, crayons, markers, colored pencils, painting sets, chalk and chalkboards; decals, games, action figures, and clothing.

☑ FUBU® **FUBU** (goods) *Owner:* GTFM, Inc. Clothing: shirts, vests, sweaters, shoes, caps, bandannas, shorts, sweatshirts, pants, belts for clothing, socks, swimwear, jackets, rainwear, blouses, dresses, footwear, hosiery, scarves, hats, headbands, pajamas, and sleepwear.

☑ Strivers Row® (goods) *Owner:* Random House, Inc. House mark for a series of fiction and nonfiction books on a variety of topics.

Choosing a Trademark

The trademark you choose is important and may be critical to the success of your business. You must answer three important questions when deciding on a trademark: first, does the trademark adequately reflect your image; second, is it available; and third, how strong is it.

Finding a Trademark That Adequately Reflects Your Image

Defining the image you want to project through your trademark is a business decision that should reflect a strategy which may follow you and your business through your lifetime and beyond. It is important for you to think about your trademark in light of the type of goods and services that you will provide, your existing trademarks, and those of your competitors. Consider these questions: Do you intend to build a series around your book or publication? Is it your persona that will drive all of your business endeavors? Have you created a captivating character in your writing? Do you want to establish a new genre that will be defined by your work? Do you want to establish your business as the source of expertise in a narrow area?

66

Seek professional help in crafting your trademark or brand as you answer these and other questions. The right trademark or brand for yourself, your business, or your work can bring great economic rewards.

Trademark Availability

A search of registered and unregistered marks, preferably by an attorney or a well-qualified search group, should be performed to find out whether the trademark you want – a word, name, logo, slogan, sound, color, design, fragrance, or some combination of those – is available. Searches can be performed at the United States Patent and Trademark Office (USPTO or PTO) Web site (http://tess.uspto.gov); however, those searches only cover trademark applications that have been filed in the PTO. It is important to search not only your proposed trademark but also variations of it. Also, for companies that market or intend to market their goods and services internationally, international (and foreign word) searches are a must.

The PTO Public Search Library for trademarks, located at Madison East Building, 1st Floor, 600 Dulany Street, Alexandria, VA, 22313, is open between 8:00 a.m. and 5:00 p.m., and use is free to the public. Also, certain information may be searched at a Patent and Trademark Depository Library. These libraries, located around the country, have CD-ROMS containing the database of registered and pending marks, but they do not show images of the design marks.

More comprehensive searches include state registries, domain names, telephone directories, databases, and periodicals. A number of commercial Internet sites provide these services. Be cautious, though; thoroughly investigate anyone you do business with on the Internet.

Preliminary Internet searches for words may be conducted using databases such as NEXIS or search engines such as Google.com, Lycos.com, Excite.com, and Yahoo.com. Domain names may be searched at http://www.internic.net/whois.html or a number of other commercial Internet sites, some free and some for a fee. The more time, money, and effort you devote to promoting your trademarked goods or services, the greater your need to search the mark thoroughly.

If you use a mark that is registered to another individual or company, that use may result in a lawsuit, with penalties ranging from stopping your use of the trademark to monetary fines. It is always better to do an extensive preliminary review and search before investing a great deal of money and other resources in marketing a trademark that may not be available or suitable for registration.

The Strength of Uniqueness

You should choose a distinctive trademark – one that is different from all known marks. Novelty carries strength. For instance, XEROX® is a distinctive trademark that had no meaning or definition until the owner created it. You can create a new word too. There are several levels of distinctiveness, ranging from fanciful (the word has no previous meaning, such as KODAK®) to arbitrary (a word that has meaning but is not associated with the goods or services offered, such as GAP® when used with clothing) to suggestive (the word has some descriptive aspect but requires some imagination to identify it with your goods and services, such as ORAL B® when used with toothbrushes).

Federal trademark registration is not available for marks that merely describe an ingredient, quality, characteristic, function, feature, purpose, or use of the relevant goods or services. An exception exists for descriptive marks that have been in existence for a long time and have developed recognition, also known as a secondary meaning.

67

Book-of-the-Month Club®, which has offered fiction and nonfiction books to its customers since 1926, is now a distinctive and strong mark. But because the mark describes the service it offers, it was probably deemed a weak mark that was not suitable for federal trademark protection until it had been in existence for five or more years, was well known in the literary community, and had developed a strong secondary meaning over time. This might explain why the application was not filed until 1948 and not registered until 1949.

A generic mark, the actual name of a good or service, is not registrable. For example, you cannot trademark the word "book" for a book, "pen" for a pen, or "computer" for a computer. Apple® is a strong arbitrary trademark for a computer, however, because its meaning has nothing to do with the product.

If a registered trademark becomes the general name for a product, over time it will lose its registered trademark status. For example, kleenex, aspirin, and band-aid were once registered trademarks that have lost their distinctiveness because they have become general product names. Any company can use these names to describe its products. But all is not necessarily lost. Owners of generic marks can use novel designs or slogans to get federal registered trademark protection, with the trademark protection limited to the new design or slogan, for marks that have otherwise lost their registration.

 Registered marks that became generic and were reclaimed through novel designs or slogans include

 Kleenex and

To protect a trademark from becoming generic, a careful strategy must be used. Often, trademark owners will monitor their marks to prevent their misuse. For instance, vendors are careful to serve only Coca Cola® when Coca Cola® or Coke® is asked for and not any other cola product because the owner of the Coca-Cola® trademark is vigilant in maintaining it and strategically watches proprietors who sell its product. The trademark owner wants to make sure that the mark is not diluted by being used to identify any and every cola product rather than Coca Cola® exclusively.

Federal Trademark Registration

Federal registration is not required to establish rights in a trademark. Common law rights arise from actual use of a mark. Generally, the first individual or entity to either use a mark in commerce or file an Intent to Use application with the PTO has the ultimate right to use and to register the mark. Also, if a trademark owner stops using a trademark, the registration ceases to exist.

Federal trademark registration has many advantages, however. It allows for

☑ constructive notice nationwide of the trademark owner's claim

☑ evidence of ownership of the trademark

☑ invoking the jurisdiction of federal courts

☑ use as a basis for obtaining registration in a foreign country

☑ filing with the U.S. Customs Service to prevent importation of infringing foreign goods

Trademark Issues Specific to Authors

A Single Creative Work versus a Series: Usually, the title of just one creative work – one book, one record or compact disc, one video, one play – may not be trademarked because the title describes the contents of that one creative work itself and does not lead you to its source or identify its source. For example, *The Good Earth, Dude, The Color Purple, A Woman's Worth*, and *Where's My Country?* are all titles of single books. Also, the name of a character in a single book is not usually thought to function as a trademark even if it forms part of the title, as Little Lulu does in *Little Lulu Goes to Market*.

When a book title acts as a single identifying source for a series, however, it then serves as a trademark for the series. Examples include *Chicken Soup for the Soul*® and *Harry Potter*®.

Pen Names: A pen name, or pseudonym, is a name a writer uses that is different from his or her legal name. Pen names, even if used in a series, do not function as trademarks.

Characters: A character from a series of books, even when used repeatedly in that series, is usually not given trademark registration. But trademark protection may be given depending on how the character is used in connection with goods. Only when the character is an identifying source for the author or the series can that character serve as a trademark. Examples include Harry Potter®, Mickey Mouse®, Nancy Drew®, and SpongeBob SquarePants®. Each immediately identifies its source of goods.

Articles, Columns, and Features in Publications: Portions or sections of publications, such as chapters or subsections of books or columns and features of newspapers or magazines, are not usually considered separate goods but are part of the publication. People usually buy the publication – the magazine, newspaper, or book – based on the mark that identifies it and not the feature or section title as the source of the information.

For example, if you read an article entitled "Self-Published Authors" in *Black Issues Book Review Magazine (BIBR)*, you are more likely to remember that you read the article in *BIBR* than to

69

remember the name of the author.

Name of Recording Artist or Group on One Recording: Similarly, the name of a recording artist or group on one recording is not registrable as a trademark for that recording. If the artist or group's name has appeared on a series of recordings, however, the artist's name or designation identifies the source and is registrable as a trademark.

 The entertainer Madonna® has trademarked her name, as have Oprah® and Iyanla®. When your name clearly identifies the source of services and goods that you provide, it is suitable for trademark protection. A trademark is a valuable property asset of the artist or author.

Online Publications: Internet publications such as e-newsletters, e-bulletins, and e-zines are a popular phenomenon. These online publications are considered a service rather than a product and are registrable under existing trademark laws.

Notable Trademark Infringement Cases

The Mid-List Case — 2004

In *Mid-List Press v. Nora,* 2004, the court found that the publishing company, Mid-List, was entitled to a permanent injunction to prevent the company president from using the company's trade name and ISBN on his book of poetry because he did not have the company's permission to use them and because such use would cause confusion in the marketplace.

The Fox News Case — 2004

An infamous lawsuit in 2004 was that of Fox News against political satirist Al Franken and Penguin for using the trademarked phrase "Fair and Balanced" in the title of Franken's book that slammed the political right.

The Playmakers LLC Case — July 15, 2004

Playmakers LLC is a sports agency that represents professional athletes. It owns two registered trademarks in the word Playmakers. ESPN is a cable network that shows sporting events and sports-related programming. In August 2003, ESPN debuted a dramatic series, *Playmakers,* a show about the behind-the-scenes happenings of a fictional football team, which was criticized by many pro players and industry professionals. Shortly thereafter, Playmakers LLC filed a trademark infringement suit and related claims against ESPN for its use of the word "Playmakers" in connection with the cable show.

In November 2003, when the first series ended, Playmakers LLC moved for an injunction to prevent ESPN from airing the show for a second series or selling it to another network or releasing the first season episodes on video. Playmakers LLC presented a "reverse trademark confusion," arguing (1) that people would view the company negatively by thinking it was infringing on ESPN's rights when in fact Playmakers LLC is the actual trademark owner and (2) that players would decline representation because of the negative critiques of the series.

The district and the appellate courts both held that the prospective clients are not likely to be confused despite the similarities and the commonness of the term "playmaker," and because of the remoteness of the parties' lines of business, the differences in their marketing channels, and the high degree of care pro athletes would likely exhibit before signing an agency deal.

The Survivor Case — September 24, 2004

Frank Sullivan, of the noted '80s rock band that released hits like "Eye of the Tiger" from the Rocky III movie, owns a registered trademark for the word "Survivor" in connection with entertainment services for band and musical services (but not merchandising). Although the group has split up and has not released new music since 1993, Sullivan continues to perform his greatest hits under the name Survivor, and to license performance rights for TV shows and commercials. Radio stations still play Survivor music and stores still sell their CDs.

In May 2000, CBS debuted its wildly successful reality TV show *Survivor*, in which sixteen participants are supposedly stranded on a remote island and must fend for themselves to survive the harsh terrain. Every few days someone is voted off the island until the last remaining participant is deemed the survivor and wins a large cash prize.

In June 2000, CBS launched a line of merchandise related to the show and, in August 2000, released a soundtrack that featured music from the show. CBS developed a Survivor logo for the show and the CD, and also used the word "Survivor" on the CD, under which was a tag line: "The Official Soundtrack to the hit CBS TV series." Another CD was released shortly thereafter.

Sullivan claims that CBS infringed his trademark by using the word "Survivor" on its CD soundtracks. To prevail, he had to prove that his rights are entitled to protection and that CBS's use creates a likelihood of confusion as to the source of the CD (that is, the band or the CBS series). The lower court found, and the Seventh Circuit affirmed, that there was no likelihood of confusion because, although the word "Survivor" was used in both cases, the band's loyal following and the show's fans would be able to differentiate between CDs from the band and those from the show. Further, CBS had taken additional measures to distinguish its CDs from the band's CDs by using tag lines that specifically reference the TV series.

71

(this page is intentionally blank—this type does NOT print)

The Anatomy of a Trademark Application

Chapter 8

You may apply for federal trademark registration in two ways:

☑ If you are already using a mark in interstate commerce – selling goods or services in two or more states – you may file an application based on that use.

☑ If you have not yet used the mark, you may file an intent-to-use application based on a bona fide intention to use it in interstate commerce. The United States Patent and Trademark Office (USPTO or PTO) will approve the mark based on that filing. But to register it, you must file an allegation of use within six months of receiving that approval. If necessary, you may file for an extension of time.

For the purpose of obtaining federal registration, *commerce* means all business or financial transactions that may lawfully be regulated by the U.S. Congress, such as commerce between states or between the United States and another country. Of course in the twenty-first century most companies will conduct business using the Internet and will market and sell to customers throughout the world, thereby meeting the use-in-commerce requirement.

 What makes a use bona fide?

Bona fide means "in good faith." Use of a mark in the ordinary course of trade, with no intent to deceive, and not only to reserve a right in a mark, is bona fide. For instance, if you live in California, selling one or two books to your cousin in Maryland may not be enough to show a bona fide use in interstate commerce, particularly if this is an advance order that you cannot ship to her yet. But if you are in the business of selling books over the Internet or through direct mail, and you sell and ship two books to your cousin in Maryland from your office in California, that would be a bona fide use.

Things to Consider before Federal Registration of Your Trademark

☑ Use of a trademark in promotion or advertising a product or service before the product or service is actually available for sale to the general public does not qualify as use in commerce.

☑ Use of a mark in local commerce within a state (intrastate commerce) does not qualify as use in commerce. But states do offer trademark protection for intrastate commerce.

Once you have determined which is the most appropriate form for you – In Use or Intent to Use – you can prepare the trademark application.

Preparing the Trademark Application

The PTO has declared that it intends to become a paperless office and has taken giant steps in that direction. In keeping with that goal, the PTO prefers that you file your application for registration of a trademark over the Internet, using the Trademark Electronic Application System (TEAS) discussed below and available at http://www.uspto.gov or on the PTO's preprinted scannable form. You may also obtain the PTO form by calling the Trademark Assistance Center at 703-308-9000 or 800-786-9199. Nonetheless, it is still good practice to keep a paper copy and transmission receipt of everything you send to the PTO, whether via snail mail or online.

The PTO strongly discourages self-created forms but will accept them if they meet the basic requirements for receipt of a filing date. (The filing date is the official indication that the PTO has not only received but has accepted your application as filed and that the review process has begun.) If you do use a self-created form, it should be on letter-size paper (8.5" × 11"), typewritten, double spaced, with margins of at least 1.5" at the left and top. The application should be written on only one side of the paper.

The Applicant: A registration application must be filed by the mark's owner or, in the case of an intent-to-use application, by the person who is entitled to use the mark in commerce. Normally, owners are the people who apply the mark to goods they produce or who use the mark in the sale or advertising of services they perform.

Applicants may be individuals or juristic persons. Juristic persons include corporations, partnerships, joint ventures, unions, associations, and other organizations capable of suing and being sued in a court of law. An operating division or the like, which is merely an organizational unit of a company and not a legal entity that can sue and be sued, may not own or apply to register a mark.

Verification: You must verify your trademark application by submitting either a signed oath or a declaration to attest to the truth of the important parts of the application and knowledge of the penalties for false statements.

A signed verification is not required for receipt of an application filing date. If the initial application does not include a proper verified statement, the PTO will require you to submit a verified statement that relates back to the original filing date.

Identifying and Classifying Goods and Services: You must include in your trademark application a list of the particular goods or services on or in connection with which you use or intend to use your mark. You should designate the appropriate international class number(s) for the identified goods or services, if you know this information. The best way to determine the international classification for your goods and services is to search a listing published online by the PTO entitled "Trademark Acceptable Identification of Goods and Services Manual" at www.uspto.gov/web/offices/tac/doc/gsmanual. (A reminder: The Web addresses given in this book are valid as of publication, but they change frequently.) The manual has an alphabetical list of goods and services and gives a classification for each item listed. It is a good practice to search registered trademarks used for similar goods or services to see what classifications they may have used.

Classifications used most often by authors:

Goods:

☑ 16. Paper goods and printed matter

Services:

☑ 35. Advertising and business

☑ 38. Telecommunications

☑ 41. Education and entertainment

☑ 42. Scientific and technological services and research and design relating thereto; industrial analysis and research services; design and development of computer hardware and software

The Bases for Filing: Before a mark will be approved for registration, an application must specify and meet the requirements of one or more of these five filing bases:

☑ use of a mark in interstate commerce

☑ bona fide intention to use a mark in interstate commerce

☑ a claim of priority, based on a foreign application filed earlier

☑ registration of a mark in the applicant's country of origin

☑ extension of protection under the Madrid Protocol

Submission of Drawings: You must submit a drawing of your trademark with your original application in order to receive a filing date, except in applications for registration of sound, scent, and other nonvisual marks. The drawing is used to reproduce the mark in the *Official Gazette* and on the registration certificate.

The main purpose of the drawing is to provide notice of the nature of the mark you want to register. The drawing is promptly entered into the automated records of the PTO and is available to the public through the Trademark Electronic Search System (TESS) on the PTO Web site at http://www.uspto.gov/main/trademarks.htm. You may submit drawings in one of two ways: special-form drawings or typed drawings.

Typed Drawings: The drawing may be typed if the mark consists only of words, letters, numbers, common forms of punctuation, or any combination of these elements. In a typed drawing, every word or letter must be typed in capital letters. Typed drawings give you a broader trademark because your application does not limit the mark to any special form or lettering. The mark in your drawing must agree with the mark as used on the specimens in your application.

Special-Form Drawings: Stylized or special-form drawings, also referred to as ink drawings, present marks that contain special characteristics, such as elements of design or color, styles of lettering, or unusual forms of punctuation. All special-form drawings must be of a quality that will reproduce satisfactorily on a black-and-white photocopier. Only black and white may appear on the drawing. If your mark includes color, it must be represented by particular patterns and shadings of gray. If the drawing is not of a quality that will reproduce satisfactorily for scanning into the PTO's database, and for printing in the *Official Gazette* and on the certificate of registration, the PTO will require a new drawing.

Specimens: You must submit a specimen, a sample that shows the mark as actually used on the goods or with the services. The specimen for a trademark for goods is a duplicate of the goods, a label or tag, commercial packaging, or a display associated with the goods bearing the trademark. If the nature of the goods makes it impractical for you to place the mark on any of those things, then documents associated with the goods or their sale may be used. Advertising, brochures, fact sheets, and telephone directories that show use of your trademark are not acceptable specimens for goods.

A specimen for your service mark application is use of your mark in the sale or advertising of your services. Service mark specimens may include newspaper, magazine, and radio ads; brochures, billboards, handbills, and direct mail leaflets; and representations of computer screens. Invoices may be acceptable service mark specimens provided they show your mark and refer to the relevant services. Letterhead, stationery, or business cards having your mark are acceptable only if the services clearly show either within the mark itself or somewhere on the paper.

Filing Costs: Your trademark application must include a filing fee for each class of goods or services that you submit, and the fee must be received before your application can be given a filing date. You may pay by credit card, check, money order, or through an existing PTO deposit account. The fee schedule is listed at the PTO site, http://www.uspto.gov/main/trademarks.htm. The fees change annually; as of this writing the filing fee is $325.00 per class if you file online and $375.00 if you file by mail.

Where to File: The application and all other correspondence should be addressed to the Assistant Commissioner for Trademarks, 2900 Crystal Drive, Arlington, Virginia 22202-3514. Trademark applications may not be filed by fax.

PTO Serial Numbers: Each trademark application received by the PTO is given a serial number that identifies it. Once the PTO assigns a serial number, you should refer to that number in all written and telephone communications about your application. The serial number is generally an eight-digit number such as 78/123456.

Enclosing a Postcard: When you submit a trademark application by snail mail it is advisable to include a stamped, self-addressed postcard with it. The postcard should specifically list each item in the mailing, namely, the written application, the drawing, the fee, and the specimens (if appropriate). The PTO will stamp the filing date and serial number of the application on the postcard to acknowledge receipt. The postcard will help you if any item is later lost or if you wish to inquire about your application. The PTO will send a separate official notification of the filing date and serial number for every application about two months after receipt.

Filing with TEAS – the Trademark Electronic Application System

The PTO has streamlined the trademark application process with TEAS, which allows you to fill out an application form and check it for completeness online. The TEAS system is divided into two parts, e-TEAS and PrinTEAS. Using e-TEAS, you can submit the application directly to the PTO online, paying by credit card, e-check, or through an existing PTO deposit account. Using PrinTEAS, you can fill in the application on the screen, print it out, and mail it to the PTO along with payment. It's your choice. Both e-TEAS and PrinTEAS are available from http://teas.uspto.gov/indexTLT.html.

Correct Use of the Symbols ™, ℠, and ®

Anyone who claims rights in a mark may use the superscript ™ (trademark) or ℠ (service mark) designation with the mark to alert the public to the claim. It is not necessary to register or even have a pending application to use these designations. Of course your claim may or may not be valid.

The registration symbol, ®, may be used only when your mark is registered in the PTO. It is improper and illegal to use this symbol at any time before the registration has been issued. Be sure to omit all symbols from the mark in the drawing you submit with your application; the symbols are not considered part of the mark. If you cannot find the ™ or ℠ symbols on your computer, change the font to superscript (under Format | Font in Microsoft Word) and type ™ or ℠.

77

Maintaining Trademark Registration

Rights in a federally registered trademark do not automatically go on forever. Registrations have an initial term of ten years. Federal registrations can last indefinitely, however, if the owner

☑ continues to use the mark on or in connection with the goods or services in the registration

☑ files all the necessary documentation in the PTO at the right time

☑ pays the requisite fees at the appropriate times

The owner of a registered mark must periodically file

☑ Affidavits of Continued Use or Excusable Nonuse, with applicable fee

☑ Applications of Renewal, with applicable fee

Forms for filing these documents are available at http://www.uspto.gov. PTO fees are adjusted annually.

Cancellation of Trademark

The PTO will not send you a notice or a reminder. To avoid cancellation of your trademark registrations, remember to put the important renewal dates in your calendar and file all required documents and fees on time.

Filing for Continued Use: Six years from the date of your registration you must file a Declaration of Continued Use, stating that you still use the mark, and you must submit specimens showing how the mark is being used. Your Declaration of Continued Use may be filed as early as year five. The PTO provides a six-month grace period after the six-year deadline to allow you to file a late declaration, for an additional late filing fee. If you fail to file a Declaration of Continued Use (Section 8 Declaration) on time, you can lose your registration and be forced to file a new application. 📄

Filing for Renewal: A renewal application, along with another Declaration of Continued Use and accompanying specimens, must be filed between the ninth and tenth year from the date of your registration. The PTO provides a six-month grace period after the ten-year deadline to allow you to file a late renewal and declaration. Renewal fees may be paid as early as year nine from the date of registration. Trademark registrations may be renewed every ten years thereafter for as long as you continue to use your mark in connection with your goods or services.

78

Registering a Trademark in a Foreign Country

Almost all countries register and protect trademarks. Each national or regional office maintains a register of trademarks that contains full application information on all registrations and renewals, and facilitates examination, search, and potential opposition by third parties. The effects of regional or national registration are, however, limited to the country or region concerned.

To avoid the need to register separately with each national or regional office, the World Intellectual Property Organization (WIPO) administers a system of international registration of marks. Two treaties govern the WIPO system: the Madrid Agreement Concerning the International Registration of Marks and the Madrid Protocol. A person who has a relationship (through nationality, domicile, or business address) with a member country of the Madrid Agreement or the Madrid Protocol, on the basis of a registration or application with the trademark office of that country, may obtain an international registration having effect in some or all of the other countries in the Madrid Union.

At present, more than seventy countries are party to one or both of the agreements. For a list of member nations, see http://www.wipo.org/madrid/en/index.html. United States trademark owners can register for trademark protection in any member country by filing a single application with the PTO.

Additionally, the United States is a member of the Paris Convention, which is a treaty relating to trademarks and other intellectual property. Each of the 140 member countries guarantees to the citizens of the other countries the same rights in trademark matters that it gives to its own citizens. The treaty also allows that on the basis of an application filed in one of the member countries, you may, within a certain period of time, apply for protection in all the other member countries.

(this page is intentionally blank—this type does NOT print)

Trademarks on the Internet
Chapter 9

As a Literary Entrepreneur, your single most important tool (outside of your creative genius) is the Internet. Whether you use it for research, marketing, e-mail discussion groups related to your literary interests, or filing your trademark application online, the Internet is essential. And most likely you'll want to have your own Web site to display and market your literary efforts. Therefore you need to know something about domain names and trademarks online.

Domain Names

A domain name, sometimes called a URL (uniform resource locator), identifies the address of a particular Web site. Your domain name may be any unique combination of letters and numerals that you choose, as long as it doesn't already belong to someone else.

Domain names are divided into two or more parts separated by a period that we refer to as a dot. The part of a domain name that precedes the last dot is called the second-level domain name; the part after the last dot is called the extension or top-level domain name. For example, in www.aol.com, the top level is com, and the second level is aol.

Top-Level Domain Names

Top-level domain names (TLDs) are the highest category and include two types: generic (gTLD) and country coded (ccTLD). No doubt you are familiar with the gTLDs that have been in use for years: com (commercial), org (organizational), edu (educational), gov (governmental), and net (network); and the more recent additions: aero, biz, coop, info, museum, name, net, org, and pro.

Six of these gTLDs — aero, biz, coop, info, museum, name, and pro — are sponsored, meaning that they are operated by specific interest groups that have established limiting criteria for use of the extensions. You can find a list of accredited registrars of domain names on the ICANN site at http://www.icann.org/registrars/accredited-list.html.

At present, more than 190 countries have their own registry authorities, each with its own operating regulations. Three examples of such ccTLDs are vg (British Virgin Islands), fr (France), and ca (Canada).

Second-Level Domain Names

The second-level domain name is where your unique name or distinct brand can appear. If the second-level domain name is distinct, then the domain name may be suitable for federal trademark registration.

 Publishers Weekly chose PublishersWeekly.com as the domain name for the company's Web site. The second-level domain name, PublishersWeekly, is the unique identifier; the gTLD, which is com, designates PublishersWeekly as a commercial entity.

Domain Names as Trademarks

There is a difference between domain names and trademarks. Domain names are unique to their owners. No two domain names are exactly the same. But they can be very similar.

 Domain names such as book.com, books.com, book-1.com, book.net, books.net, book.org, and books.org could coexist.

On the other hand, trademark law allows two or more trademarks to exist for the same mark as long as they are in different classes.

 For the trademark Amazon:

AMAZON — International Class 11: Water softening units for domestic use owned by Aquion Corporation.

AMAZON — International Class 35: Electronic retailing services via computer, featuring books, music, videotapes, compact discs, floppy disks, and CD-ROMs, owned by Amazon.com, Inc.

AMAZON — International Class 30: Breakfast cereals owned by Nature's Path Foods Inc.

AMAZON — International Class 32: Non-alcoholic carbonated and non-carbonated soft drinks owned by Laurel Hill, Inc.

82

To properly act as a trademark or service mark, your domain name must actually be used in connection with the associated goods or services in addition to serving as a domain name. If the domain name is used only as an Internet address, that use will not give trademark or service mark rights. On the other hand, a mark that has been given trademark or service mark rights through actual or constructive use can be used as a domain name provided it affords a unique Internet address. For example, in BlackVoices.com® the second level domain name, BlackVoices, is used in connection with associated services, including an e-zine, in addition to serving as the Internet address for BlackVoices.com.

The PTO will not register domain names in which the second-level name is not unique. For example, books.com, pens.com, and furniture.com could not be registered as trademarks because the words in their second-level names (books, pens, furniture) are generic.

The prefixes e- and i-, indicating electronic and Internet, are not protectable as trademarks unless the word they accompany is unique and not descriptive or generic. For example, eBook.com is a generic name for a book and therefore is not suitable for registration of any goods or services actually dealing with books; on the other hand, iUniverse.com® is unique and arbitrary terminology for a book publisher and therefore is suitable for trademark or service mark registration.

Domain Name Disputes

Cybersquatting: Domain name disputes have arisen largely from the practice of cybersquatting, which involves the registration of trademarks and brand names of established companies and individuals by third parties as domain names. Since registration of domain names is simple and inexpensive – usually under $40 US – cybersquatters use the opportunity to register hundreds of trademarks or brand names as domain names. As the holders of these domain names, cybersquatters often put them up for auction or offer them for sale directly to the company or person involved, at prices much more than the cost of domain registration. They also may keep the domain name and use the good reputation of the person or business associated with it to attract business for their own sites.

Typosquatting: Similar to cybersquatting, the practice of typosquatting involves the registration of trademarks and brand names with an intentional typo; perpetrators count on the statistical probability of typographical errors to divert traffic to a site completely unrelated to the trade-marked company's site. For example, typosquatters commonly drop the last letter of a domain name (Unite.com instead of United.com). This is an unscrupulous tactic to lure business to illegitimate Web sites. Originally, there was no agreement within the Internet community that would allow organizations which register domain names to prescreen the filing of potentially problematic names. The reasons included the stimulation of business as well as First Amendment rights of freedom of expression and difficulties in determining ownership rights in a name or brand. Over time, more disputes and litigation between the cybersquatters and trademark owners evolved. Today, with the new classes of top-level domains, a number of prescreening alternatives are being tested and used to discourage cybersquatting and typosquatting activity.

Dispute Resolution: Two major vehicles have come into existence to settle domain name disputes: the Uniform Domain Name Dispute Resolution Policy (UDRP) and the Anticybersquatting Consumer Protection Act (ACPA).

ICANN, the organization responsible for, among other things, management of the generic top-level domains, recognized the urgent need to solve the dispute-resolution problem. A system of internationally uniform and mandatory procedures to deal with what are frequently disputes across borders was sought.

With the support of its member states, the World Intellectual Property Organization (WIPO), which is mandated to promote the protection of intellectual property worldwide, consulted extensively with members of the Internet community around the world. Using information from a WIPO report containing recommendations dealing with domain-name issues, ICANN adopted UDRP.

UDRP: This policy went into effect on December 1, 1999, for all ICANN-accredited registrars of Internet domain names. UDRP permits complainants to file a case with a resolution service provider, specifying

- ☑ the domain name in question
- ☑ the respondent or holder of the domain name
- ☑ the registrar with whom the domain name is registered
- ☑ the grounds for the complaint

Such grounds include the way in which the domain name is identical or similar to a trademark to which the complainant has rights; why the respondent should be considered as having no rights or legitimate interests in respect to the domain name that is the subject of the complaint; and why the domain name should be considered as having been registered and used in bad faith.

These disputes have been decided overwhelmingly in favor of the trademark holder, and thus cybersquatting and typosquatting have been extinguished in large part. The process is quick and cost-efficient. Legitimate questions still arise that require dispute resolution. For example, more than one person may have the same registered trademark for a different product or industry; therefore each has a legitimate right to have the domain name.

ACPA: On November 29, 1999, ACPA was enacted by the United States Congress and became a part of the Lanham Act. ACPA gives trademark holders greater leverage with cybersquatters and an ability to protect their interest in their trademarks. ACPA has provisions for injunctive relief and statutory damages. It is another weapon to use against cybersquatters and typosquatters, and is similar to UDRP in its effect.

In a recent case, Retail Services, Inc. filed a suit in federal court for a declaratory judgment that its use of www.freebie.com did not infringe on Freebies Publishing's trademark in the word "Freebies" primarily because the word "freebie" was generic and not entitled to trademark protection, and thus did not violate ACPA by cybersquatting and did not infringe on the company's trademark. The defendant countersued for, among other things, trademark infringement and trademark dilution because its mark, Freebies®, was a registered mark. The court held that the word "freebies" was generic and therefore not registrable as a federal trademark, and thereafter the court ordered the defendant's registration to be canceled.

Meta Tags

Meta tags are special types of HTML (HyperText Markup Language) tags that provide information about Web pages. Three particularly important meta tags are described below.

Title: The title meta tag is the short title of your Web site, which is displayed in the Web browser heading.

Description: The description meta tag is a short comment that informs search engines about what can be found at the site.

Keyword: The keyword meta tag is designed to alert Web search engines to those terms the author of the site or the webmaster considers especially important, and to draw users to the site.

Search engines such as Google, Lycos, and Yahoo! create their various indexes from a review of the meta tags contained within a Web site. Therefore, Web page authors will include meta tags in the HTML and use terms, including trademarks, that they think will attract users. Webmasters often repeat keywords many times so that the search engines will rank their Web site over those of their competitors.

> Authors of Web pages will often include the trademark of competitors in their keyword meta tags, thereby hoping to attract users who are trying to locate Web sites associated with their competitors' trademarks. Many courts have prohibited these practices.

Trademarks are valuable assets. They symbolize the goodwill that Literary Entrepreneurs have established with their customers, clients, and the marketplace at large through their goods or services. In fact, trademarks may be the most valuable assets of your business. It is critical to select, use, register, maintain, and protect your trademarks because the life of your business and your future success may depend on it.

85

(this page is intentionally blank—this type does NOT print)

A Brief History of Intellectual Property Law

Chapter 10

In 2002, the United States Congress noted that copyright-based industries represent one of the most valuable economic assets of this country, contributing more than 5 percent of the gross domestic product. In addition, the intellectual property sector employs approximately 4,300,000 people, representing more than 3 percent of total United States employment. Apart from their economic benefits to society, literary and artistic contributions have proved to be an integral part of individual, community, and societal success. Thus, intellectual property remains as important in today's society as it was when the drafters gathered to create the constitutional right of an author to control how his or her writings, art, or discoveries are used. This right is deeply rooted in American law. As stated in the U.S. Constitution, article I, section 8:

> The Congress shall have Power . . . To promote the Progress of Science and useful Arts, by securing for limited Times to Authors and Inventors the exclusive Right to their respective Writings and Discoveries.

Copyright and trademark laws are of particular interest and concern to writers because they are integrally related to the writing process.

The History of Copyright Law

One of the first enactments of copyright law occurred on May 31, 1790. Congress has since made several substantial revisions to the law.

Act of 1909

The first major revision occurred in 1909 and was codified in 1947 as Title 17 of the Copyright Act. The 1909 act required strict adherence to the formalities of copyright notice, registration, and renewal. Therefore, works that were otherwise protectable could fall into the public domain if any of the formalities were not satisfied. The 1909 act continues to apply to works created before January 1, 1978.

> Care should be taken if a new work, otherwise governed by the Revised Act of 1976, incorporates parts of a prior work that is governed by the 1909 act.

Act of 1976

The 1909 act was substantially revised in 1976. This first version of the 1976 act (see below for the revised version) — also commonly referred to by writers and publishers as the Act of 1989 —

applies to works created between January 1, 1978, and February 28, 1989, and those years are known as the Decennial Era of Copyright Law. While somewhat less stringent than the 1909 law, the 1976 act still required authors to adhere to certain formalities of notice and registration, and denied copyright protection for any works that failed to comply, moving them into the public domain.

Act of 1976 Revised

In 1989, Congress revised the 1976 act to amend certain provisions so that United States copyright law would comply with the Berne Convention for the Protection of Literary and Artistic Works. The Berne Convention is an international copyright treaty that requires all signatories to eliminate the requirements for notice and registration as a condition of copyright protection. Formalities like notice and registration are still important, however, because works created after 1978 and before 1989 are governed by the original version of the 1976 act.

One of the most prominent and important concepts recognized and protected by the Berne Convention is the concept of moral rights. The term "moral rights" (or *droit moral*) encompasses the right of attribution and the right of integrity. The right of attribution ensures that artists are properly identified with the works they create and are not associated with works they did not create. The right of integrity prevents the intentional distortion, mutilation, or other modification of a work of art that injures an artist's honor or reputation.

Moral rights are personal to the author and therefore may not be transferred to another person. Moral rights may be waived, however, by a written document signed by the author. Moral rights have been recognized for many years in most European countries and in other signatory nations of the Berne Convention, but not explicitly by the United States.

When Congress amended the 1976 act, it expressly declared that the Berne Convention protections are not self-executing (not automatically incorporated by reference into U.S. law), that claims arising under the Berne Convention must be handled according to the existing laws of the United States, and that no further rights beyond those expressly included by amendment are recognized. The practical effect of these declarations was that Congress declined to adopt the moral rights provisions of the Berne Convention, stating that the rights of attribution and integrity were sufficiently protected under existing federal, state, and local laws. That conclusion was challenged and ultimately addressed, in part, in 1990.

Visual Arts Rights Act of 1990

Realizing the inconsistency between United States copyright law and the Berne Convention in regard to moral rights, Congress enacted the Visual Arts Rights Act (VARA) to grant visual artists, such as painters and sculptors, the rights of attribution and integrity for certain one-of-a-kind and limited-edition prints of visual art works.

In the 2001 case *Flack v. Friends of Queen Catherine, Inc.*, the federal district court in the Southern District of New York held that a grossly negligent or intentional modification of a work of visual art may be actionable under VARA.

The passage of VARA was the first instance in which the United States recognized and expressly granted moral rights, but Congress did so in a very limited way. VARA extended moral rights protection to visual artists who create paintings, drawings, limited prints, sculptures, and still photographs produced for exhibition purposes only. The Copyright Act enumerates several limitations and requirements that allow the work of a visual artist to enjoy the protections of moral rights. For more information about VARA, see www.copyright.gov/title17/92chap1.html#106a (general provisions) and www.copyright.gov/title17/92chap1.html#113 (scope of rights and exception for artwork incorporated into buildings).

Digital Millennium Copyright Act

Congress enacted another significant amendment to the Copyright Act, the Digital Millennium Copyright Act (DMCA), which President Clinton signed into law on October 28, 1998. The DMCA is made up of the World Intellectual Property Organization (WIPO) Copyright Treaty, the WIPO Performances and Phonograms Treaty, the Online Copyright Infringement Liability Limitation Act, the Computer Maintenance Competition Assurance Act, and the Vessel Hull Design Protection Act. Although specific discussion of these various acts is well beyond the scope of this book, you should know that the DMCA sought to bring the body of copyright law in line with unique technological advances like software and the Internet. As it did with the Berne Convention, Congress made it clear that DMCA was not self-executing and that no further rights were granted other than those expressly provided in the law.

For purposes of this book, suffice it to say that the DMCA generally makes it illegal to circumvent anti-piracy measures or to manufacture, sell, or distribute circumvention devices. The DMCA also provides exemptions to certain entities like libraries and educational institutions under certain circumstances, and limits the liability of Internet Service Providers (ISPs) and online service providers (like universities) for copyright infringement of users (provided they have an anti-infringement policy, take reasonable steps to implement the policy, notify users of the policy, and take down the offending material after receiving notice of the infringement).

89

The History of Trademark Law

Unlike patent and copyright law, federal trademark law has no constitutional provision that expressly permits its development. The basis for the federal trademark law is the Commerce clause in the U.S. Constitution, article I, section 8, which states in part:

The Congress shall have the power to regulate Commerce
with foreign Nations, and among the several States ...

Under the authority of the Commerce clause, Congress passed the Lanham Act (found at 15 USC. §§1051 et seq.) to establish a federal system of trademark registration. Congress also decided that the United States Patent and Trademark Office would administer the regulation of trademarks on a national level.

The Lanham Act not only ensures the nationwide protection of trademarks but protects against deceptive practices in marketing goods and services. If you couple federal trademark law with state common law and state statutory law, you will find that you have several alternatives for registering and protecting your trademarks.

Pending Legislation
Affecting Authors
Chapter 11

Bill Number	Title	Date of Introduction
S. 2560	Inducing Infringement of Copyrights Act of 2004	6/22/2004
H.R. 4077	Piracy Deterrence and Education Act of 2004	3/31/2004
S. 2237	Protecting Intellectual Rights Against Theft and Expropriation Act of 2004	3/25/2004
S. 1932	Artists' Rights and Theft Prevention Act of 2004	11/22/2003
H.R. 2752	Author, Consumer, and Computer Owner Protection and Security (ACCOPS) Act of 2003	7/16/2003
H.R. 2601	Public Domain Enhancement Act of 2003	6/25/2003

Inducing Infringement of Copyrights Act of 2004 (S. 2560)

S.2560 amends the current Copyright Act and states that whoever intentionally induces any copyright infringement shall be liable as an infringer.

The *Congressional Record* states, "This legislation is also carefully crafted to preserve the doctrine of 'fair use.' Indeed by targeting the illegal conduct of those who have hijacked promising technologies, we can hope that consumers in the future have more outlets to purchase creative works in a convenient, portable digital format. Similarly, the bill will continue to promote the development of new technologies as it will not impose liability on the manufacturers of copying technology merely because the possibility exists for abuse. Finally, the bill will not affect Internet service providers who comply with the safe harbor provisions of the Digital Millennium Copyright Act."

The bill "protects the rights inherent in creative works, while helping to ensure that those same works can be easily distributed in digital format."

Piracy Deterrence and Education Act of 2004 (H.R. 4077)

Congressman Lamar Smith introduced H.R. 4077 to enhance criminal enforcement of the copyright laws, to educate the public about the application of copyright law to the Internet, and more. The purpose was to respond appropriately to the reality that the most popular publicly accessible peer-to-peer file sharing software programs, combined, have been downloaded worldwide more than 600,000,000 times and that the abuses of such technology (trading pornography, spreading viruses, and copyright infringement, to name a few) threaten the viability of the otherwise beneficial aspects of peer-to-peer technology. On September 29, 2004, this bill was received in the Senate.

Protecting Intellectual Rights Against Theft and Expropriation Act of 2004 (S. 2237)

S. 2237 gives the attorney general (AG) the power to initiate a civil action against anyone who engages in copyright infringing activities. The bill includes specific civil penalties and allows the AG to collect statutory damages and damages and profits resulting from infringement. The bill includes two other directives: the AG will (1) develop a program for qualified personnel from the Department of Justice and U.S. Attorneys' Offices that will train them to implement new policies of copyright law enforcement, and (2) the AG will report annually to Congress on the progress made in implementing the training programs and enforcement.

Artists' Rights and Theft Prevention Act of 2004 (S. 1932)

Senator John Cornyn found that federal legislation was necessary to combat the most egregious forms of online theft of intellectual property and its significant, negative economic impact on the national economy. Therefore, he introduced S. 1932 to provide criminal penalties for unauthorized recording of motion pictures in theaters and other similar facilities, and to provide criminal and civil penalties for unauthorized distribution of commercial prerelease motion pictures. Among other things, this bill allows facility owners or their employees to detain suspected infringers until law enforcement arrives. It also establishes criminal copyright enforcement penalties and allows the preregistration of certain works.

Author, Consumer, and Computer Owner Protection and Security (ACCOPS) Act of 2003 (H.R. 2752)

Congressman John Conyers introduced H.R. 2752, which enhances domestic and international enforcement of the existing copyright laws, to encourage creative people to develop and distribute creative works. Specifically, the bill requires the attorney general to report to Congress annually on criminal copyright infringement cases and to share information with foreign authorities regarding individuals who may be involved in infringing activities. Also, it establishes criminal penalties for the unauthorized uploading of copyrighted work to computer networks, for any person offering file sharing software without warning the user about privacy and security risks for using such software, and for an individual who provides false information in a domain registration or who illegally records a motion picture in a theater.

On September 4, 2003, this bill was referred to the Subcommittee on Courts, the Internet, and Intellectual Property. No further action has been reported.

Public Domain Enhancement Act of 2003 (H.R. 2601)

Congresswoman Zoe Lofgren introduced H.R. 2601 to amend existing copyright law in order to institute a renewal or maintenance fee for copyrights. Under her proposed legislation, you would have a copyright term of fifty years, and then you could extend it for ten years each time you renewed it. If you did not renew by the end of any term, you would lose your copyright and the work would fall into the public domain.

Congresswoman Lofgren asserted that the existing copyright term, which runs for the life of the author plus seventy years after his or her death, is too long and therefore is contrary to the intent and purpose of the Copyright Act, which, according to the congressional findings, "was not intended to deprive the public of works when there is no commercial or copyright purpose behind their continued protection."

(this page is intentionally blank—this type does NOT print)

Contracts Basics
Chapter 12

Every contract, whether written or oral, includes three basic elements: the offer, the acceptance, and the consideration.

A contract is a legally enforceable agreement between two or more legally competent parties – individuals, businesses, or other organizations – in which one party makes an offer to do or refrain from doing something, the other accepts the offer, and each exchanges something of value, also called consideration. Consideration is a legal concept best described as the benefit or detriment that induces someone to make a promise and enter into a contractual arrangement based on the terms, conditions, rights, and obligations agreed to by the parties involved.

Contracts are legally enforceable only if there is sufficient consideration to show that each party has given something of value to benefit from the deal. For example, if A offers to print B's books for $2,000, and B accepts by giving A $2,000 for the printed books, and A gives B the printed books, each gives something of value.

By contrast, an offer and acceptance without adequate consideration is merely a gift. For instance, if A offers to give B $10, and B accepts but makes no promise in return, then A's transfer of $10 to B is a gift and not a legally enforceable contract. The practical effect is that generally speaking, B cannot sue A to pay the $10 if A reneges on her promise. But in some cases a court will enforce an agreement made for less than adequate consideration if one party relied to his or her disadvantage on the promise of another. This is known in legalese as detrimental reliance.

> A contract is void if the promise on which it is based is illegal or illicit. For example, an agreement between two drug dealers about the exchange of money for drugs is not legally enforceable because the promises involve the completion of an illegal act.

A valid contract must contain the material terms – the most important terms – of the agreement: the who, what, where, when, how, and how much of the mutual benefits and obligations. Collectively, these essential terms govern the transaction.

> **????** If it's not in writing, it's not a legally enforceable contract.
>
> This assumption is false. An oral agreement can be enforceable in court if the basic contract elements exist and the essential terms are mutually agreed upon. But certain contracts are legally required to be in writing. Contracts are governed by state law, which of course differs from state to state. Nonetheless, each state has a Statute of Frauds which requires that certain contracts be in writing. In most cases, the following contracts must be in writing:
>
> wills
>
> ☑ sale of real property

☞ lease of property with a term of more than one year

☞ contracts with a term of more than one year or a value above a certain amount

Nonetheless, to be prudent, it is best to put all agreements in writing to have records of them and to avoid misunderstandings and miscommunications.

Breach of Contract and Damages

When one party fails to perform his or her obligations under the contract, this is known as a breach of the contract, and the non-breaching party may sue to enforce the terms of the contract and collect damages (although other remedies short of filing a lawsuit may be effective). The premise of damages is to make the non-breaching party "whole," that is, restored to his or her position before entering into the agreement. This premise is different from criminal penalties that seek to punish and to reform behavior.

In most cases, the non-breaching party will receive monetary damages. Sometimes, however, money will not make the non-breaching party whole. For example, when an author licenses her article to a magazine for first serial print publication rights, but the publisher also posts the article on its Web site without obtaining electronic rights, the author may sue for monetary damages (statutory damages if he or she was savvy enough to have registered the copyright within three months of publication). But the author may also not want the article posted online for a variety of reasons. In fact, getting the magazine to remove the article from its Web site may be more valuable to the author than any amount of money he or she may be entitled to recover. Therefore, the author may, in addition to money damages, demand equitable damages in the form of an injunction to force the magazine publisher to remove the article from the Web site.

The following are the various damages and other remedies available:

☞ **Compensatory Damages:** Money damages to compensate the non-breaching party for the amount of the loss.

☞ **Consequential and Incidental Damages:** Additional money damages to compensate the non-breaching party for other costs associated with the breach that were reasonably anticipated (even if not actually anticipated) by all parties when they entered the contract.

☞ **Attorney Fees and Costs:** Recovery of the costs of litigation by the non-breaching party if included in the terms of the contract.

☞ **Liquidated Damages:** Monetary damages expressly provided for in the terms of the contract; usually included when actual monetary damages would be difficult to determine if a breach occurred.

☑ **Specific Performance:** A court order for the breaching party to perform as agreed to in the contract; not applicable to contracts to sing or write, for instance, because this requirement would in effect be indentured servitude (working against one's will); but applicable to contracts involving, for example, the transfer of unique property.

☑ **Punitive Damages:** Money awarded only in the most egregious contract cases to deter the breaching party and others from repeated occurrences of the wrongdoing; almost never awarded in contract cases.

☑ **Rescission:** When the contract is terminated and both parties are excused from further performance.

☑ **Reformation:** When the contract is revised to properly reflect the original intentions of the parties.

Defenses to a Claim of Breach of Contract

Even when breach of contract is established, a defendant may avoid liability by proving at least one of the most common legal defenses:

☑ **Lack of Consideration:** At least one party did not give something of value to the other party. As a result the transfer is considered a gift instead of a legally enforceable contract.

☑ **Duress, Undue Influence, Fraud:** One party was under significant pressure (give me your money, or I'll kill you) or was tricked into signing the contract.

☑ **Lack of Competence:** One of the contracting parties was a minor (minors cannot enter into contracts) or was mentally incapable of entering into a legally enforceable contract.

☑ **Impossibility:** Through no fault of either party, something unforeseeable, such as an act of God, terror, or war, occurred that made it impossible to perform under the terms of the contract.

☑ **Illegality:** The terms of the contract were illegal, making the contract legally unenforceable.

97

(this page is intentionally blank—this type does NOT print)

The Publishing Agreement

Chapter 13

In simple terms, a publishing agreement ▤ (also referred to as a book deal or contract) is a legal arrangement between an author and publisher. The author agrees to transfer to the publisher certain rights in the bundle of rights associated with her copyrighted manuscript, and the publisher agrees, in turn, to pay for the costs to publish the manuscript. In exchange, both parties receive some financial gain (the publisher reaping the lion's share, of course). By agreeing to pay for all costs of publishing (in the best-case scenario), in effect the publisher becomes an investor in the author's manuscript. The publisher is entitled to recoup the initial investment and to take a sizeable percentage of the income generated by sales and licensing of the work. The author often receives an advance against royalties (explained below) and a percentage of royalties and subsidiary rights income.

Many complaints are hurled at publishers for the seemingly unfair percentages of income and the extensive rights they retain in publishing deals. But the publishing industry, like any industry, is very much a bottom-line business. And it is often a challenge for publishers to make profits because the majority of publishing agreements do not earn out, meaning that most publishers (small and big alike) do not earn back their initial investment, which includes the author's advance. This advance is a payment to the author before publication; it is offset by income from sales after publication; in other words, it's a loan from the publisher to the author.

Generally, publishers create a Profit and Loss Statement to anticipate the costs of publication (prepress, printing, marketing, and promotion) and projected earnings, taking into account the proposed market and demand for the book, industry discounts of at least 50 percent, and returns of at least 20 percent. Based on the net profit number, publishers select a figure they reasonably believe they will recoup from sales and, in most cases, pay the author an advance based on some percentage of that anticipated profit. A book earns out when all costs, including the advance, are recouped from sales and licensing revenue.

99

But it is not uncommon for a book to go out of print after selling only 5,000 copies. Imagine the following scenario: You sign an agreement with a major publishing company in New York for hardcover rights to your fiction manuscript. You receive a modest $60,000 advance and a standard royalty schedule of 10 percent for the first 5,000 copies sold. If the net retail price is $24.95, gross profit on 5,000 copies would be $124,750. Applying the average industry discount of 50 percent reduces net profits to $62,375. Now apply the loss of income for returns of 20 percent, which reduces the net profits to $49,900. Subtract $20,000 in production costs (not including your advance), and $29,900 remains. Your royalty of 10 percent yields $2,990, against which your author advance is applied, and the publisher is still in the hole to recoup the remaining $57,010 paid in advance to you.

But do not cry for the publisher just yet because it does pocket $26,910. In addition, the example does not account for the licensing of subsidiary rights like book club rights, mass market rights, audio book rights, electronic rights, and so forth. The point is that the publishing industry is a dollars-and-cents business from the publisher's perspective. And despite your core values as a creative spirit who values words over profits, if you intend to be successful in this business, you must begin to understand and embrace the bottom line too.

Why You Need a Written Contract

It is critical to put the agreement between author and publisher in writing because the terms and conditions determine what rights are transferred, what compensation you and the publisher receive, when the rights revert back to you, and what state law governs the contract if a disagreement develops. You should never leave these issues to oral agreements or handshake deals. Always get it in writing and make sure the contract states clearly what each party agrees to do and what each will receive in return.

Now hear this, authors: You do a disservice to yourself, given your hard work and considerable talents, when you dot every "i" and cross every "t" in your manuscript but rush through a publishing agreement, often without the guidance of an experienced literary lawyer, and sign it without negotiating the terms from a position of knowledge and strength. Or worse yet, you fail to ensure that all material terms are negotiated favorably and stated clearly in a written agreement signed by you and the publisher.

In the days and weeks leading up to the signing of a publishing agreement, when the publisher has declared interest in your manuscript but you have not yet committed yourself in writing, you are in the strongest position from which to negotiate. And these negotiations are most important because your contract defines what rights you are transferring, what (if any) rights you keep, how your agent and publisher get paid, and how you get paid. Keep in mind that what you agree to today affects you and the other party or parties for years to come. Don't you think that is worth taking seriously and slowly?

Consider this: although a certain author advance and royalty schedule may seem great now, how fair will it be when you are a best-selling author yet still earning pennies on each book sold while the publisher has long since recouped its investment and is still raking in the lion's share of the profits? Or perhaps transferring all of your rights to a publisher may seem like a good idea now. But what if the publisher does not have any intention of using some of the rights or is actually in no better position than you to properly exploit them? Why transfer them in the first place? This is especially true since it may be more financially beneficial to divide the rights and sell them to a number of different buyers then to lump them together and sell to one buyer.

The point is that there is no such thing as a nonnegotiable contract. Do not sign a contract with anyone who tells you there is. Everything is up for discussion. Compare this process to other areas of your life and ask yourself, "Would I just sign any paper given to me if I were buying a house or car, or making a long-term investment, or going into a long-term business relationship with someone I just met?" I venture to guess that your answer to these questions would be no, and that you would take care to read the document and consult with someone more knowledgeable than you to make sure the rights and responsibilities of both parties were set forth clearly and that you were getting not only what is fair but what is in your best interest, to the greatest extent possible.

The most common fear authors have when faced with a deal is the dreaded *fear of negotiation*. In the spirit of not wanting to offend, many authors in first-time bargaining situations shy away from asking hard questions and requesting more favorable provisions. Worse still, some authors are intimidated by the process and the documents. That, coupled with an author's excitement over the possibility of any deal, after receiving so many rejections, is a dangerous mix that often spells trouble. Authors do not want to challenge the agent or publisher because they do not want to be perceived as difficult or money hungry. But remember, this is a bottom-line business, and the operative word is "business." Agents and publishers have their own attorneys, and so should you. Any reputable person in the industry understands that offers should be negotiated by competent professionals; it's just business.

The Contract Terms

There are as many variations in the precise terms of a publishing agreement as there are publishing agreements. But certain key terms should exist in every contract. This section focuses on key clauses in a standard publishing agreement. You will find a complete sample form in Appendix B and in the Forms Library on the CD.

Understanding the nature, purpose, meaning, and effect of the key clauses in the contract is an important first step in breaking down complex legal terminology into common understanding. Of course, literary law is a vast and complex subject. Accordingly, this section is merely a broad overview of some of the most common and essential clauses in a publishing agreement. Compare the discussion that follows to the corresponding clause in the sample contract.

Introductory Paragraph: Most contracts begin with an introductory paragraph that sets forth the names and legal capacities of the parties as well as the effective date of the agreement. It may also include their addresses.

⊙━🔑 This Agreement is made this _____ day of _____, 2005 (The Agreement), by and between _____, an individual (hereinafter referred to as AUTHOR) located at _____, and ABC Publishing Company, a corporation (hereinafter referred to as PUBLISHER) whose principal place of business is located at _____, concerning a work presently entitled _____ (as described in greater detail below).

Description of the Work: The Description of the Work clause, although simple to understand, is a clause to which you should pay close attention. In many cases the description is basic and general, providing an approximate page length or a specified number of words, the general topic, and the tentative title. But you should consider including more information or incorporating the book proposal and perhaps sample chapters as an attachment (known as an Exhibit) to the agreement. This revision is important to consider if the publisher has the right to reject the manuscript and terminate the agreement if it is not "acceptable to the publisher in form and content" (see Delivery and Acceptance sections below). If the publisher has this right to reject, you need to be reasonably certain that your understanding of what the manuscript will contain is consistent with the publisher's expectation of what you will submit. Problems can result when the publisher's expectations for the manuscript differ from the author's understanding. Therefore, sometimes a more detailed description benefits both parties.

⊙━🔑 Delivery and Acceptance of the Manuscript

Author shall deliver to Publisher on or before _____, 2005 (the Delivery Date), one (1) original hardcopy of the complete Work and one (1) copy on computer disk, together with any supplementary materials (including, without limitation, drawings, illustrations, photographs, maps, graphs, tables). If Author fails to deliver the Work by the delivery date, after a grace period of thirty (30) days (or such other period as shall be determined by the Publisher and agreed to in writing by both parties), Publisher may demand the return of all sums paid to or on behalf of Author by Publisher in connection with the Work, and this Agreement shall terminate. Upon termination under these circumstances, Author may not resubmit the Work (or any part thereof) or a similar work to any other publisher without first offering it to Publisher under the same terms contained in this Agreement.

Publisher shall inform the Author in writing as to whether the complete Work is acceptable to Publisher in form and content within ninety (90) days of receipt of the complete Work. If Publisher determines the Work is unacceptable but capable of cure, Publisher and Author shall agree upon a time for revision (Revision Period) and Publisher shall provide to Author written comments explaining the necessary revisions. If Publisher determines that the first submission cannot be cured or that the revision created during the Revision Period is still unacceptable, Publisher shall have the right, in Publisher's sole discretion, to reject the Work by giving written notice to the Author.

If the Work is rejected, Author shall keep fifty percent (50%) of the advances paid to date and shall return the remaining fifty percent (50%) within one year of rejection. The Author may submit the Work to a third party, provided that Author shall remain obligated to repay to Publisher the amounts retained by Author from all proceeds from any sale of license by the Author of rights of any nature in the Work to a third party (the First Proceeds).

The clauses dealing with delivery and acceptance of the manuscript are important and sometimes problematic parts of the contract.

Delivery: The contract should spell out the date that the manuscript is due and in what form or forms (hardcopy, e-mail attachment, disk) it should be delivered, as well as any technical specifications (margin width, one-sided, double-spaced) required by the publisher. In addition, any supplementary materials expected to accompany the manuscript (photographs, illustrations, and other materials created by someone else – that may require permissions) should be noted in this section.

Supplementary Materials and Indexing

Be sure to check the fine print in the contract about supplementary materials (photographs, illustrations, artwork, interview excerpts, and so forth). If your work includes supplementary materials, a publisher will require that you get permission from the owner to use them. Also, if you transferred to an agent rights that you intend to give to the publisher, you will need permission from the agent to do so (often covered by an agency clause inserted into the contract). Lastly, if your work needs an index, the publisher will require either that you provide it when you deliver your complete manuscript (or sometime thereafter as agreed to) or that you pay for the expense of having the index written.

First, confirm whether you are responsible for (1) obtaining and (2) paying for supplementary materials. Generally publishers require in the contract that authors seek and pay for the cost of obtaining permissions, although sometimes the publisher will agree to actually obtain permission since it may be in a better position to do so. Publishers will also ask you to pay for illustrations, artwork, maps, indexing, and so forth. But these requirements can (and should) be negotiated so that either the publisher pays or the costs are split between publisher and author. If you cannot change the terms, try to get the publisher to advance you the money and to recoup its expenses from your royalty account so that you do not have to pay any out-of-pocket expenses.

For a sample permissions form, see Appendix B.

103

Acceptance: At times a publisher or an editor at a large publishing company will offer a book deal in response to a query letter, proposal, or pitch. Based on that material, the editor will formulate certain expectations of the final manuscript. If those expectations are not adequately spelled out in writing and conveyed to the author, the finished product will not be what the editor expected.

Another possibility is that although the editor conveys his or her expectations clearly, the author, who was great at crafting a pitch, is ill equipped to finish the manuscript. To deal with these contingencies, publishers often demand that the manuscript be delivered in a form and content satisfactory to the publisher. Clearly, this is subjective and gives a publisher wide latitude to reject a manuscript. Some authors negotiate for a more objective clause that sets forth criteria that, if met, will render the manuscript fit for publication. An alternate approach is to give the author the opportunity to cure the defect (revise the manuscript) based on the publisher's comments.

⚷ Grant of Rights

> The Author hereby grants, transfers, and assigns to the Publisher for the full term of copyright the exclusive right to publish in hardback and paperback editions (the Primary Rights) and sell throughout the world in the English language the literary work presently entitled _____ (hereinafter called Work). The Author also grants and assigns to the Publisher the exclusive subsidiary rights to said Work, with exclusive authority to license said rights in all countries and in all languages.

This clause defines the rights the author will assign to the publisher, the nature of the rights, the applicable territory, and the amount of time the contract will remain in effect (but see the section "Reclaiming Your Copyright after Transfer" in chapter 2). The assignment of rights means that the publisher and not the author is the owner of whatever rights are conveyed during the term of the agreement. Generally, the grant of rights is exclusive to one publisher. Sometimes authors assign the entire bundle of rights by way of a broad, all-inclusive grant of rights such as the one noted in the sample clause, but you need not transfer all of your rights to the publisher. And you should always include a reservation-of-rights clause after the grant of rights as follows:

> ⚷ All rights not expressly granted to the Publisher are hereby reserved by the Author.

Keep in mind that if you have or intend to have a Web site in the future, you should consider reserving rights in your domain name, and protecting your ability to sell author copies (watch for a clause that restricts your ability to sell author copies) and to provide information from your Web site with no limitation by or compensation to the publisher.

In addition, you should only grant to a publisher the rights you believe the publisher is capable of exploiting to your benefit. A publisher may, as a matter of course, seek to control all rights. But why grant motion picture or dramatic rights, for instance, if the publisher has neither successfully exploited those rights in the past nor has established relationships in those fields to exploit the rights successfully in the future. Although licensing motion picture or dramatic rights is speculative in most cases, it may be best to retain them and sell them to others who are in a better position to successfully exploit them. The point is, do not just go along simply for the sake of appearing agreeable. And even if you cannot negotiate to keep certain sub-rights, you can use them as a bargaining chip to negotiate other clauses to your advantage.

Some authors negotiate a more limited grant of rights for a particular work (for example, the hardcover rights, paperback rights, mass market rights, book club rights, foreign rights, large print rights, and a host of others). Doing so allows the author to shop the remaining rights and negotiate a deal (based on the strength of the first edition) with the same publisher or with a different one. The grant of rights can also be limited by language (for example, the English-speaking market) or by territory (North America only, for example).

Secondary (or Subsidiary) Rights: Ordinarily, the primary right granted to a book publisher is the right to publish the manuscript in book form. This right can include all print rights or, for instance, only hardback, trade paper, or mass market rights. Some publishers however, seek electronic, spoken-word edition, Internet, audio, and book club rights in the primary grant. Traditionally, these rights were considered subsidiary or secondary to the primary right to publish the manuscript in book form. But as new media are developed and used to publish works in other forms, publishers will more aggressively try to control all known and future uses. Case law, however, suggests that unless the rights are expressly stated, they will not be transferred, which runs contrary to the "future media" clause in most publishing agreements.

You (or your agent, if you've transferred the rights to the agent) may also assign secondary or subsidiary rights to the publisher so that the publisher can exploit the Work in ways that may be less important (but still valuable) to the publisher, such as mass market paperback rights, book club rights, and foreign and translation rights, and in media other than books, such as motion picture and television rights, stage plays (dramatic rights), electronic rights, performance rights, and more. Again, keep in mind that any of these rights could be included in the primary rights clause if the publisher primarily intends to exploit them. Therefore the subsidiary rights list below is not etched in stone but serves as a guide for your information.

Subsidiary rights include

- ☑ Periodical rights (first or second serial)
- ☑ Book club rights
- ☑ Dramatic rights (theatrical rights)
- ☑ Motion picture and TV rights
- ☑ Videocassette and audiocassette rights
- ☑ Radio rights
- ☑ Merchandising (commercial tie-in) rights
- ☑ New technology
- ☑ Foreign translation rights
- ☑ Electronic rights
- ☑ Internet rights
- ☑ Mass market paperback rights

One of the most important sections of a publishing contract deals with how you get paid. A publishing company can compensate an author in several different ways; sometimes the publisher uses one particular method of payment; at other times two or more methods are combined.

Advance: A more apt title for this clause would be "loan" because, as the word suggests and as stated above, this payment is an advance against future royalties. The advance is commonly paid in three installments, one-third on signing, one-third on delivery, and one-third on acceptance (or publication), although there are several variations on this theme, including half on signing and half on publication.

Royalties: Royalties are payments made by the publisher to the author based on money received from sales. Think of a royalty as a percentage of every book sale. Royalties do not ordinarily include monies earned from licensing agreements for the exploitation of subsidiary rights, as defined above.

Royalties are generally based on the retail price of the book. Royalty calculations can include escalations that attach higher rates to greater numbers of books sold. Additionally, some publishers opt to have separate royalty calculations for different editions. Typical escalations based on the U.S. cover price may look like this:

Hardback	Trade Paper	Mass Market Paperback
10% on first 5,000	8% on first 10,000	6 to 8% on first 150,000 copies
12.5% on next 5,000	10% on all additional copies	8 to 10% on all additional copies
15% on all additional copies		

As stated above, publishers traditionally base the royalty rate on the retail or cover price. This is the price printed on the book. But a significant number of publishers have moved away from tradition and instead base royalty rates on the net price, which is the price actually received by the publisher. This break in tradition has occurred because of the rise of mandatory discounts within the industry to booksellers (20 to 40 percent), distributors (50 to 55 percent), and wholesalers and book clubs (as much as 60 percent).

When negotiating your royalty rate, try to secure a bonus structure for receiving what we call professional recognition. Professional recognition can be placement on a prominent best-seller list (*New York Times*), a literary prize that ultimately increases sales (Pulitzer), or any other honor, award, or achievement, such as signing a motion picture or TV deal.

Net Revenues: Sometimes publishers offer a percentage of net revenues instead of a sales royalty and licensing percentage scheme. This is most likely to be offered by independent publishers, who try to avoid the administrative hassles that accompany complex royalty calculations. Instead, the publisher will recoup its expenses and then split the remaining revenue based on a negotiated percentage.

Flat Rate: Although this is not a common option, some publishers offer a flat fee to purchase your manuscript. This may occur, for instance, in writing competitions where the prize is a lump sum plus publication, or for contributions to an anthology that are being paid for with money and not just with copies of the finished book.

Options: The options clause gives the publisher the first right to purchase (or refuse) the next work created by the author. A typical options clause might look like this:

> Publisher shall have the right to acquire Author's next book-length work on terms to be mutually agreed upon by the parties. Author shall submit a detailed outline and sample chapter of the next book-length work to Publisher before submitting the work to any other publisher, and Publisher shall have a period of thirty days after receipt of said detailed outline and sample chapter (the Option Period) in which to review the submission and determine whether to exercise the option. The Option Period shall not begin to run earlier than sixty days after publication of the Work. If Publisher declines or fails to exercise its option by the expiration of the Option Period, then Author may submit the work to other publishers or otherwise dispose of the work, at Author's sole discretion.

Note that in the example the publisher has the right to purchase the next work on terms "to be mutually agreed upon by the parties." But most option clauses will state that the publisher can acquire the next work on the same terms as the existing agreement. If that is the case, the same option clause (and advance and royalty rates) will appear in the second contract and the third and so on, until the publisher decides not to exercise its option. So the two-book deal winds up being a multiple-book deal for the publisher, without an opportunity for the author to negotiate a more favorable deal based on success of the first or second book.

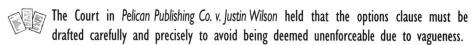 The Court in *Pelican Publishing Co. v. Justin Wilson* held that the options clause must be drafted carefully and precisely to avoid being deemed unenforceable due to vagueness.

107

Of course the publisher wants as many opportunities as possible not only to recoup its sizable investment but also to benefit financially from the success of the work. On the other hand, you want to be in a position to negotiate a more lucrative and favorable deal if the initial work is successful. Therefore, this is an extremely important clause that should be negotiated carefully and comprehensively.

A sub-rights compensation clause could look like this:

> The net revenues received from the exploitation of the enumerated subsidiary rights shall be shared fifty percent (50%) to the Author and fifty percent (50%) to the Publisher, except that the division of the net revenues from dramatic, motion picture, and television licenses shall be seventy-five percent (75%) to the Author and twenty-five percent (25%) to the Publisher.

Revisions: The revisions clause is not appropriate for fiction, but appears for most nonfiction books. At first glance, many authors are put off by the revisions clause. But in reality, revising nonfiction keeps the information fresh and can extend the shelf life of the book. But you must take care to limit the revisions clause and to insert some protective provisions that seem to be conspicuously absent from most publishing agreement drafts (to the great detriment of the author). Those provisions appear in bold in the box below.

> The Author shall revise the Work (a Revised Work) **two (2) times** after initial publication and within one (1) year from the receipt of written request from the Publisher to do so. A Revised Work shall not substantially alter the original Work and further, **shall not constitute a new work for copyright and royalty escalation purposes.** In the event that the Author is unable or unwilling to provide a revision within one (1) year after the Publisher has requested it, or should the Author be deceased, the Publisher may have the revision made **at the Publisher's expense** (such expense to be recoupable from royalties) and may display, in the revised Work and in advertising, the name of the person or persons who perform the revision.

This clause, as drafted, builds in certain protections for authors. First, it limits the number of revisions. Second, it states that a revision will not be considered a new work for purposes of copyright term and royalty escalations. Authors do not want the term or number of books sold to begin from zero again. Third, authors should try to negotiate to have the publisher pay for the costs of revisions if the author does not or cannot revise the work when requested to do so.

Out-of-Print/Reversion Clause: The out-of-print clause is extremely important for several reasons. First, the definition of the term "out-of-print" determines when the rights revert back to the author; that is, when all rights in copyright of the published work are transferred back to the author from the publisher. Second, because of electronic publishing, including e-books, print-on-demand technology, online services, and interactive media, it can now be argued that the work will never go out of print because the electronic files and print-on-demand technology are not capable of being exhausted. Unfortunately, many publishing agreements are used over and over again without being updated to reflect current conditions. Therefore, a new definition of "out-of-print" must be included in publishing agreements today to account for new technologies and to protect authors.

108

> The Work shall be considered to be out of print if it is not available in the United States through regular retail channels in the English language book form edition and not listed in the publisher's catalog; further availability through print-on-demand or other electronic or mechanical means alone does not make a book in print. In the event that the Publisher fails to keep the Work in print and the Author makes a written request of the Publisher to keep the Work in print, the Publisher shall, within sixty (60) days after receipt of that written request, notify the Author in writing of the Publisher's decision in the matter. If the Publisher elects to keep the Work in print, it shall have six (6) months thereafter to reprint and release the Work into ordinary sales channels. In the event that the Publisher elects not to keep the Work in print or fails to comply

with the deadline of six (6) months (unless the failure is due to circumstances beyond its control), then this agreement shall terminate and all rights granted to the Publisher shall revert immediately to the Author.

Special clause to address electronic versions of the Work

If Publisher sells no more than _____ copies of Author's Work in either electronic or downloadable format, or by means of print-on-demand technology, over any _____ consecutive-month period of this Agreement, then either party may terminate this Agreement upon thirty (30) days' notice in writing sent to the other party. Upon such termination, all rights granted under this Agreement, except the rights to dispose of existing stock including but not limited to electronic, printed, or audio copies, shall revert to Author, subject to all rights that may have been granted by Publisher to third parties under this Agreement, and Publisher shall have no further obligations or liabilities to Author except that Author's earned royalties shall be paid when and as due.

A Publisher's Duty to Publish: A publisher's duty to publish must be specifically addressed in the agreement. This includes what damages the author will receive if the publisher fails to publish as promised. The court in *Alternative Thinking Systems Inc. v. Simon & Schuster* suggested that authors should receive, at a minimum, all advances paid to date and immediate reversion of rights. What would happen if the author has not received an advance remains an unanswered question.

Agent Clause: If you have an agent who has gotten you a publishing deal, there will be a paragraph in the publishing agreement appointing the agent as your representative to collect monies and to receive notices on your behalf. While this may seem like a standard innocuous clause, I caution writers to be on the lookout for what the Author's Guild has called the "interminable agency" clause.

In "Avoid Granting an Interminable Right to Represent Your Work," an article e-mailed to members on May 11, 2004, the Author's Guild warned authors to avoid the interminable agency clause. This clause, which often appears in the agency paragraph in a publishing agreement (but not in the author–agent agreement, in most cases), gives agents the exclusive right to receive royalties from works covered by the agreement for the entire term of copyright. At present, the term of copyright lasts for the life of the author plus seventy years.

109

The Author's Guild lists a number of valid reasons why this clause does not benefit either party. One of the most obvious and important reasons from an author's perspective is that an agent's rights should run co-extensively and co-terminously with the publishing agreement and should terminate when a work goes out of print, when presumably the benefit of the agent's work also ends. Of course most authors do not begrudge an agent's right to a commission when it is earned through the agent's substantial efforts to place a work with a publishing house. But giving any further compensation to the agent without a new rights sale, license, or other exploitation of the author's work, is at best unfair and, in my opinion, borders on unconscionable.

As agents see it, they work on commission, and some literary properties sell quickly while others take a considerable amount of time and effort to shop. So agents will try to protect their interests by increasing their opportunity to recoup their investments and make a living. Nonetheless, there are so many ways an author can successfully challenge such a clause that the agent could easily spend more time embroiled in conflicts (and even litigation) with clients then he or she does making deals and finding new clients. And tracking and enforcing interminable rights for each client over many years seems to be an administrative burden and, quite frankly, an impossibility when it is unlikely the agency will even be in existence for the entire term of copyright (again, the author's life plus seventy years). Thus the cons seem to far outweigh the pros when you think about the small amount of compensation (if any) that may be earned and paid to an agent after a work goes out of print.

So I recommend that authors and agents make sure that the agency paragraph in publishing agreements no longer includes the interminable agency clause, also known as a right coupled with an interest.

Publishing Agreement Checklist: A comprehensive publishing agreement will have all thirty of the following clauses:

- ☑ Recitation
- ☑ Grant of Rights, including
  - Description of the Work and Rights Granted
  - Territory
  - Language
  - Term
- ☑ Reservation of Rights
- ☑ Delivery and Acceptance of Work
- ☑ Additional Materials
- ☑ Permissions
- ☑ Representations and Warranties
- ☑ Duty to Publish
- ☑ Artistic Control
- ☑ Compensation Scheme (advance, royalties, net revenues, and so forth)
- ☑ Subsidiary Rights
- ☑ Payments
- ☑ Accounting
- ☑ Inspection of Books

☑ Copyright

☑ Indemnity

☑ Free Copies

☑ Revisions

☑ Reversion

☑ Remaindering

☑ Successors and Assigns

☑ Termination

☑ Agent Clause (if author has an agent)

☑ Promotion and Use of Author's Persona & Likeness

☑ Arbitration

☑ Notice

☑ Entire Agreement

☑ Waiver and Default

☑ Governing Law

☑ Signature Lines

(this page is intentionally blank—this type does NOT print)

Other Important Agreements
Chapter 14

Although the publishing agreement usually receives a lot of attention, you should be aware, as a Literary Entrepreneur, that other contracts relating to the publishing industry may also be significant for you. In fact, before entering into a publishing agreement with you, a publisher may ask you for copies of a collaboration agreement (if you worked with others to create your book) and a licensing agreement (if you have incorporated the work of others – pictures, illustrations, photographs, and so forth – in your book). In addition, many writers enter into an agency agreement before ever receiving a publishing contract; therefore the agency agreement is also a very important document to become familiar with and to understand.

The Collaboration Agreement

Although the writer's life is often solitary, sometimes two or more people decide to contribute to one work. This situation can be a blessing or a curse depending on how you set up your professional relationship with your collaborators; so if you intend to work with someone else to create a joint work, you should consider entering into a collaboration agreement.

A collaboration agreement ▤ is used when two or more people contribute to a book; the contributors may be, for example, two authors or an author and an illustrator. The collaboration agreement sets forth the understanding between the parties involved regarding the nature of the work, their business relationship, what they will each contribute, what percentage of revenue for the book each will receive, and so forth. The agreement should

☑ describe the work

☑ describe each person's contribution, the schedule of anticipated due dates, the form in which the contribution should be submitted, and the arrangements regarding how the contributors will share all financial and other responsibilities to develop the work

☑ state how long the collaboration agreement will remain in effect and, if the term expires or the contract is terminated, which, if any, clauses will remain in effect

☑ outline what happens if one of the contributors should become physically or mentally incapacitated or die during the term of the agreement

☑ set forth how artistic decisions will be made, namely, whether each contributor shares artistic control over the entire project, whether each person has individual control over his or her contribution, or whether one person has the final say about all such decisions

☑ state how business decisions will be made, namely, whether all contributors have a say, whether there will be a majority vote, or whether one contributor controls all business decisions

☑ describe what happens if or when offered an agency or publishing agreement (to the extent the contributors do not have an agent or the publishing agreement isn't already entered into)

☑ discuss how and when intellectual property rights will be applied for or registered

☑ address how derivative works will be managed

☑ enumerate what financial investment each party will make, whether expenses and investments will be recoupable and how revenues will be divided, and whether contributors receive income individually or whether one person collects on behalf of everyone and then distributes payments

☑ set forth how contributors will be credited in the work and in advertisements and publicity related to the work

☑ address the circumstances under which the agreement can be terminated

☑ declare what law shall apply in the case of a dispute and whether the parties must submit to arbitration

☑ include any other provisions that further define the rights and responsibilities of the contributors

The Agency Agreement

An agency agreement is (usually) a straightforward and succinct document that details the rules which will govern your relationship with the agency as long as the agreement is in force. It is particularly important to understand that the terms you agree to today will be the ones you will be required to follow for a long, long time. So, even if the contract is only a few pages long, you must take the time to go over every word. Ask questions of all the professionals involved in the transaction. And contact a lawyer to review the terms with you and negotiate the most favorable terms for you so that you can live with them comfortably over the long term.

The basic terms provide that you designate the agent or agency as your exclusive agent to represent your rights (either all rights or only those limited rights set forth in the agreement), for a specific period of time referred to as the term of the agreement, in a specific area referred to as the territory; that all money owed to you from the sale of your rights will be sent first to your agent; and that he or she (or the agency) is entitled to a percentage, known as the commission, of that compensation – usually 10 to 20 percent of your gross receipts (with the average being 15 percent) – before he or she distributes the remainder to you.

Although there is some disagreement (usually from newly formed or small agencies) about whether writers should pay any fees to agents, it is generally considered unethical for a writer to have to pay any reading fees (monthly, annually, or otherwise). But reimbursement or advance payment of extraordinary expenses may be appropriate (for travel, hand-delivery charges, or anything above and beyond ordinary business expenses). The agency business is a risk–reward business; the agent is supposed to make an up-front investment in your work in order to earn 10 to 20 percent of your hard-earned money for as long as the book exists, which she will earn if her efforts are successful and she sells your book. So writers beware; make sure any fees are warranted.

At a minimum, the agency agreement should include

☑ a clear and specific transfer-of-rights clause that details the rights given to the agent, the length of time the transfer lasts (term), the area that the agreement covers (territory, such as regional, national, international, world), and which rights you are reserving for yourself (or an "all rights not specifically mentioned are hereby reserved ..." clause)

☑ amount of the agent's commission, whether it is based on gross or net compensation, and the deadline by which the agent must pay you the amounts due to you

☑ what, if any, expenses you are responsible for

☑ author and agent representations and warranties, especially that the agency will use its "best efforts" to sell the author's work

☑ power of attorney clause granting the agent the right to collect money on your behalf and to endorse checks, and to deduct the agency commission from that money

☑ assignment provisions

☑ termination provisions

☑ accounting, author statements, and auditing provisions

☑ a provision that indicates what law applies to interpret and enforce the agreement

Watch for automatic renewal provisions and negotiate them carefully or strike them altogether. And be sure to exclude any pre-existing deals you have with publishers from the deals covered by the agency agreement.

The Licensing Agreement

A licensing agreement ▤ sets forth terms that permit others the limited right to use your work. In contrast to an assignment (such as that in a publishing contract) where you, as the copyright owner, actually transfer the copyright to a new owner (the publisher), in a license you retain the copyright but give permission to the licensee to use the work in a certain way, for a certain time, and in a specified area.

The license should

- ☑ describe with great specificity the property to be licensed
- ☑ note the date the property will be delivered to the licensee and in what form it must be delivered
- ☑ describe with great specificity the rights granted to the licensee, namely, setting forth exactly how the licensee is allowed to use the property and whether those rights are exclusive or nonexclusive
- ☑ note the language and geographical locations in which the property can be used and how long the license will remain in effect
- ☑ include a reservation-of-rights clause stating that any use not expressly granted in the license is reserved by you
- ☑ set forth the payment terms, which may include a lump sum license fee, advance, royalty schedule, license fees paid in installments, and so forth
- ☑ include provisions for copyright notice and credit
- ☑ address whether the licensee has the right to alter the property in any way
- ☑ include a confidentiality clause for any proprietary information disclosed to the licensee regarding the property or your business pursuits
- ☑ outline the ways each party can terminate the agreement
- ☑ discuss whether parties must submit to arbitration in case of a dispute
- ☑ discuss whether the license can be assigned by any party
- ☑ include the governing law
- ☑ include a no-agency clause

You should make sure that the license is comprehensive enough to secure rights in all intended uses. The *New York Times*, *Newsday*, and *Time Magazine* (print publishers) and NEXIS and University Microfilms International (UMI) (electronic publishers) learned this lesson the hard way. On June 25, 2001, in *New York Times et al. v. Tasini et al.*, the Supreme Court in a seven-to-two decision upheld the rights of Jonathan Tasini, Mary Kay Blakely, Barbara Garson, Margot Mifflin,

Sonia Jaffe Robbins, and David S. Whitford, all freelance writers, to require the print and online publishers involved to acquire the right to include their copyrighted works in electronic databases that store information in a text-only format.

The authors, all of whom worked as independent contractors, individually transferred to at least one of the print publishers first serial rights in his or her article to be included in a collective work (the newspaper or magazine). The publishers licensed the text of articles appearing in their publications to NEXIS – and the *Times* (but not *Newsday* or *Time*) also licensed *Times* materials to UMI to reproduce those materials on two CD-ROM products – to include in the electronic database. Through a computerized retrieval system, database users sign on to their account (or access the CD-ROM), and search the database for files by author, subject, date, publication, headline, key term, words in text, or other criteria. In response to the input information, the search agent scans the database and provides the user with a list of all the articles that meet the search criteria. The user can view, print, or download the individual articles, which are displayed with information about the print publication, publication date, section, initial page number, headline or title, and author. But individual articles are not linked to the other articles with which they appeared in the collective work; rather, each stands alone. The authors registered their individual copyrights and the publishers registered their copyrights in their collective works.

The writers alleged in their original complaint that their copyrights had been infringed by the inclusion of their articles in the databases, and they sought declaratory and injunctive relief, and monetary damages. In response, the publishers argued that they were entitled to reproduce and distribute the articles because of the privilege given to collective-work copyright owners.

The Court disagreed with the publishers and concluded that the databases could not be considered collective works because the articles stood alone rather than in the context of the entire work (magazine or newspaper) or any revision of the work (a special edition), or even as a later work within the same series (a "where are they now" piece). Thus the Court ruled that the publishers infringed the copyrights of the freelance authors.

There are many critical points in *Tasini*; however, as it pertains to licensing agreements, the ruling demonstrates that the electronic publishers believed they had the right to use the literary property transferred from the print publishers. In fact they did not. In retrospect, of course, the electronic publishers should have required the print publishers to attach the necessary permissions to use the individual works. As you can see, the expense of not getting the proper permissions to use copyrighted work turned out to be far greater than that of obtaining the permissions beforehand.

Since the first edition of *Literary Law Guide for Authors*, several federal courts have interpreted *Tasini*, with some interesting and diverging results. One such case to actually go against freelancers

117

in a copyright and trademark infringement case is *Faulkner et al. v. National Geographic Society et al.* (2003). The freelancers in that case contributed articles or photographs to *National Geographic* under various contractual agreements to appear in the magazine's print version. In 1997, *National Geographic* used the contributions in its CD-ROM and DVD digital archive on CD-ROM and DVD to cover all issues from 1888 to 1996 and titled *The Complete National Geographic: 108 Years of National Geographic.*

The freelancers argued that *National Geographic*'s use of their works infringed their copyrights and violated their rights with respect to their original contributions since copyright in the individual article or photograph belongs to the freelancer. On the other hand, *National Geographic* owns a copyright in the entire collective work and, pursuant to copyright law, has the right to make, reproduce, and distribute the contributions as part of the collection and to revise the collection.

The fundamental issue in the original court case was whether *National Geographic*, owner of the copyright in the magazine issues that included the freelancers' contributions, is privileged by section 201(c) of the Copyright Act that allows copyright owners of collective works to reproduce and revise the original work. *National Geographic* argued that the use was proper and privileged because its use of the freelancer contributions was purely archival and without manipulation or alteration, much like a microfilm or microfiche reproduction. The freelancers won the original case, relying in part on a 2001 decision against the magazine decided in the Court of Appeals for the Eleventh Circuit with the same facts and issues as those in *Faulkner,* but on appeal, *National Geographic* prevailed. The court of appeals decided that the images that made up *The Complete National Geographic* were all virtually identical to the original issues.

Resources for Writers
Appendix A

Resource	Contact
Web Sites	
Copyright Clearance Center	www.copyright.com, not to be confused with copyright.gov (the official Copyright Office Web site listed below).
Copyright Office	www.copyright.gov
FindLaw.com: an online database of helpful legal resources on many different areas of the law	www.FindLaw.com
Intellectual Property Owners Association	www.ipo.org
Internet Corporation for Assigned Names and Numbers (ICANN)	www.icann.org
Legal Information Institute of Cornell University	www.law.cornell.edu
Library of Congress	www.loc.gov
United States Patent and Trademark Office (PTO)	www.uspto.gov
World Intellectual Property Organization (WIPO): an international organization focused on protecting the rights of intellectual property owners	www.wipo.org
Conferences	
BookExpo America	www.bookexpoamerica.com
Frankfurt Book Fair	www.frankfurt-bookfair.com
Harlem Book Fair	www.qbr.com
Horror Writers Association Annual Conference	www.horror.org/conference.htm
Infinity Publishing	www.infinitypublishing.com/conferences1.htm
Latino Book & Family Festival	www.latinobookfestival.com

Maui Writers Conference	www.mauiwriters.com
Romance Writers Association Annual Conference	www.rwanational.org
Shaw Guides: perhaps the most comprehensive listing of conferences available on the Internet	http://writing.shawguides.com
Writers Conference at Penn	http://www.sas.upenn.edu/CGS/ cultural/writersconf/index.php

Organizations

Association of Authors and Publishers	www.authorsandpublishers.org
National Association of Women Writers	www.naww.org
National Writers Union	www.nwu.org
Publishers Marketing Association (PMA)	www.pma-online.org
Small Publishers, Artists, and Writers Network	www.spawn.org
Small Publishers Association of North America (SPAN): an organization whose mission is "to advance the image and profits of independent publishers through education and marketing opportunities"	www.spannet.org
Women's National Book Association	www.wnba-books.org
Writer's Guild of America	www.wga.org

Magazines

Black Issues Book Review	www.bibookreview.com
ForeWord Magazine	www.forewordmagazine.net
Poets & Writers	www.pw.org
Publishers Weekly	www.publishersweekly.com
Quarterly Black Review	www.qbr.com
The Writer	www.thewritermagazine.com
Writer's Digest	www.writersdigest.com

Forms
Appendix B

Copyright
TX (Literary Works)

Copyright Office fees are subject to change. For current fees, check the Copyright Office website at *www.copyright.gov*, write the Copyright Office, or call (202) 707-3000.

Form TX
For a Nondramatic Literary Work
UNITED STATES COPYRIGHT OFFICE

REGISTRATION NUMBER

TX   TXU

EFFECTIVE DATE OF REGISTRATION

Month   Day   Year

DO NOT WRITE ABOVE THIS LINE. IF YOU NEED MORE SPACE, USE A SEPARATE CONTINUATION SHEET.

1

TITLE OF THIS WORK ▼

PREVIOUS OR ALTERNATIVE TITLES ▼

PUBLICATION AS A CONTRIBUTION If this work was published as a contribution to a periodical, serial, or collection, give information about the collective work in which the contribution appeared.   **Title of Collective Work ▼**

If published in a periodical or serial give: Volume ▼   Number ▼   Issue Date ▼   On Pages ▼

2 a

NAME OF AUTHOR ▼

DATES OF BIRTH AND DEATH
Year Born ▼   Year Died ▼

Was this contribution to the work a "work made for hire"?
☐ Yes
☐ No

AUTHOR'S NATIONALITY OR DOMICILE
Name of Country
OR { Citizen of ▶
Domiciled in ▶

WAS THIS AUTHOR'S CONTRIBUTION TO THE WORK
Anonymous?   ☐ Yes ☐ No
Pseudonymous? ☐ Yes ☐ No

If the answer to either of these questions is "Yes," see detailed instructions.

NATURE OF AUTHORSHIP Briefly describe nature of material created by this author in which copyright is claimed. ▼

NOTE

Under the law, the "author" of a "work made for hire" is generally the employer, not the employee (see instructions). For any part of this work that was "made for hire" check "Yes" in the space provided, give the employer (or other person for whom the work was prepared) as "Author" of that part, and leave the space for dates of birth and death blank.

b

NAME OF AUTHOR ▼

DATES OF BIRTH AND DEATH
Year Born ▼   Year Died ▼

Was this contribution to the work a "work made for hire"?
☐ Yes
☐ No

AUTHOR'S NATIONALITY OR DOMICILE
Name of Country
OR { Citizen of ▶
Domiciled in ▶

WAS THIS AUTHOR'S CONTRIBUTION TO THE WORK
Anonymous?   ☐ Yes ☐ No
Pseudonymous? ☐ Yes ☐ No

If the answer to either of these questions is "Yes," see detailed instructions.

NATURE OF AUTHORSHIP Briefly describe nature of material created by this author in which copyright is claimed. ▼

c

NAME OF AUTHOR ▼

DATES OF BIRTH AND DEATH
Year Born ▼   Year Died ▼

Was this contribution to the work a "work made for hire"?
☐ Yes
☐ No

AUTHOR'S NATIONALITY OR DOMICILE
Name of Country
OR { Citizen of ▶
Domiciled in ▶

WAS THIS AUTHOR'S CONTRIBUTION TO THE WORK
Anonymous?   ☐ Yes ☐ No
Pseudonymous? ☐ Yes ☐ No

If the answer to either of these questions is "Yes," see detailed instructions.

NATURE OF AUTHORSHIP Briefly describe nature of material created by this author in which copyright is claimed. ▼

3 a

YEAR IN WHICH CREATION OF THIS WORK WAS COMPLETED   This information must be given
◀ Year in all cases.

b DATE AND NATION OF FIRST PUBLICATION OF THIS PARTICULAR WORK
Complete this information ONLY if this work has been published.
Month ▶ _____ Day ▶ _____ Year ▶ _____   ◀ Nation

4

See instructions before completing this space.

COPYRIGHT CLAIMANT(S) Name and address must be given even if the claimant is the same as the author given in space 2. ▼

TRANSFER If the claimant(s) named here in space 4 is (are) different from the author(s) named in space 2, give a brief statement of how the claimant(s) obtained ownership of the copyright. ▼

DO NOT WRITE HERE
OFFICE USE ONLY

APPLICATION RECEIVED

ONE DEPOSIT RECEIVED

TWO DEPOSITS RECEIVED

FUNDS RECEIVED

MORE ON BACK ▶   • Complete all applicable spaces (numbers 5-9) on the reverse side of this page.
• See detailed instructions.   • Sign the form at line 8.

DO NOT WRITE HERE
Page 1 of _____ pages

EXAMINED BY	FORM TX
CHECKED BY	
☐ CORRESPONDENCE Yes	FOR COPYRIGHT OFFICE USE ONLY

DO NOT WRITE ABOVE THIS LINE. IF YOU NEED MORE SPACE, USE A SEPARATE CONTINUATION SHEET.

PREVIOUS REGISTRATION Has registration for this work, or for an earlier version of this work, already been made in the Copyright Office?
☐ Yes ☐ No If your answer is "Yes," why is another registration being sought? (Check appropriate box.) ▼
a. ☐ This is the first published edition of a work previously registered in unpublished form.
b. ☐ This is the first application submitted by this author as copyright claimant.
c. ☐ This is a changed version of the work, as shown by space 6 on this application.
If your answer is "Yes," give: **Previous Registration Number** ▶   **Year of Registration** ▶

5

DERIVATIVE WORK OR COMPILATION
Preexisting Material Identify any preexisting work or works that this work is based on or incorporates. ▼

Material Added to This Work Give a brief, general statement of the material that has been added to this work and in which copyright is claimed. ▼

a
6
b

See instructions before completing this space.

DEPOSIT ACCOUNT If the registration fee is to be charged to a Deposit Account established in the Copyright Office, give name and number of Account.
Name ▼   **Account Number** ▼

CORRESPONDENCE Give name and address to which correspondence about this application should be sent.   Name/Address/Apt/City/State/ZIP ▼

a
7
b

Area code and daytime telephone number ▶   Fax number ▶
Email ▶

CERTIFICATION* I, the undersigned, hereby certify that I am the
Check only one ▶
- ☐ author
- ☐ other copyright claimant
- ☐ owner of exclusive right(s)
- ☐ authorized agent of _____

of the work identified in this application and that the statements made by me in this application are correct to the best of my knowledge.

Name of author or other copyright claimant, or owner of exclusive right(s) ▲

8

Typed or printed name and date ▼ If this application gives a date of publication in space 3, do not sign and submit it before that date.

_____   Date ▶ _____

Handwritten signature (X) ▼

X _____

Certificate will be mailed in window envelope to this address:	Name ▼
	Number/Street/Apt ▼
	City/State/ZIP ▼

YOU MUST:
Complete all necessary spaces
Sign your application in space 8
SEND ALL 3 ELEMENTS IN THE SAME PACKAGE:
1. Application form
2. Nonrefundable filing fee in check or money order payable to *Register of Copyrights*
3. Deposit material
MAIL TO:
Library of Congress
Copyright Office
101 Independence Avenue, S.E.
Washington, D.C. 20559-6000

Fees are subject to change. For current fees, check the Copyright Office website at www.copyright.gov, write the Copyright Office, or call (202) 707-3000.

9

*17 U.S.C. § 506(e): Any person who knowingly makes a false representation of a material fact in the application for copyright registration provided for by section 409, or in any written statement filed in connection with the application, shall be fined not more than $2,500.

Rev: June 2002 20,000   Web Rev: June 2002 ♻ Printed on recycled paper   U.S. Government Printing Office: 2000-461-113/20,021

Copyright
TX Short Form

Copyright Office fees are subject to change. For current fees, check the Copyright Office website at *www.copyright.gov*, write the Copyright Office, or call (202) 707-3000.

Short Form TX
For a Nondramatic Literary Work
UNITED STATES COPYRIGHT OFFICE

REGISTRATION NUMBER

	TX		TXU

Effective Date of Registration

Application Received

Examined By

Deposit Received	
One	Two

Correspondence ☐

Fee Received

TYPE OR PRINT IN BLACK INK. DO NOT WRITE ABOVE THIS LINE.

Title of This Work: Alternative title or title of larger work in which this work was published:	**1**	
Name and Address of Author and Owner of the Copyright: Nationality or domicile: Phone, fax, and email:	**2**	Phone ( ) Fax ( ) Email
Year of Creation:	**3**	
If work has been published, Date and Nation of Publication:	**4**	a. Date _____ _____ _____ *(Month, day, and year all required)* Month Day Year b. Nation
Type of Authorship in This Work: Check all that this author created.	**5**	☐ Text (includes fiction, nonfiction, poetry, computer programs, etc.) ☐ Illustrations ☐ Photographs ☐ Compilation of terms or data
Signature: Registration cannot be completed without a signature.	**6**	*I certify that the statements made by me in this application are correct to the best of my knowledge.* Check one: ☐ Author ☐ Authorized agent X _
OPTIONAL **Name and Address of Person to Contact for Rights and Permissions:** Phone, fax, and email:	**7**	☐ Check here if same as #2 above. Phone ( ) Fax ( ) Email

8 Certificate will be mailed in window envelope to this address:

Name ▼

Number/Street/Apt ▼

City/State/ZIP ▼

Complete this space only if you currently hold a Deposit Account in the Copyright Office.

9 Deposit Account #_____
Name _____
_____
_____

DO NOT WRITE HERE   Page 1 of _____ pages

*17 U.S.C. § 506(e): Any person who knowingly makes a false representation of a material fact in the application for copyright registration provided for by section 409, or in any written statement filed in connection with the application, shall be fined not more than $2,500.

Rev: August 2003—30,000   Web Rev: August 2003   ⊕ Printed on recycled paper

U.S. Government Printing Office: 2003-496-605/60,027

Copyright Office fees are subject to change.
For current fees, check the Copyright Office
website at *www.copyright.gov*, write the Copyright Office, or call (202) 707-3000.

FORM PA
For a Work of the Performing Arts
UNITED STATES COPYRIGHT OFFICE

REGISTRATION NUMBER

PA   PAU

EFFECTIVE DATE OF REGISTRATION

Month   Day   Year

DO NOT WRITE ABOVE THIS LINE. IF YOU NEED MORE SPACE, USE A SEPARATE CONTINUATION SHEET.

1
TITLE OF THIS WORK ▼

PREVIOUS OR ALTERNATIVE TITLES ▼

NATURE OF THIS WORK ▼ See instructions

2 a
NAME OF AUTHOR ▼

DATES OF BIRTH AND DEATH
Year Born ▼   Year Died ▼

Was this contribution to the work a
"work made for hire"?
☐ Yes
☐ No

AUTHOR'S NATIONALITY OR DOMICILE
Name of Country
OR { Citizen of _____
Domiciled in _____

WAS THIS AUTHOR'S CONTRIBUTION TO
THE WORK
Anonymous?   ☐ Yes ☐ No
Pseudonymous?   ☐ Yes ☐ No

If the answer to either
of these questions is
fiYes, see detailed
instructions.

NATURE OF AUTHORSHIP Briefly describe nature of material created by this author in which copyright is claimed. ▼

NOTE

Under the law,
the fiauthor of
a fiwork made
for hire is
generally the
employer, not
the employee
(see instruc-
tions). For any
part of this
work that was
fimade for hire
check fiYes in
the space
provided, give
the employer
(or other
person for
whom the work
was prepared)
as fiAuthor of
that part, and
leave the
space for dates
of birth and
death blank.

b
NAME OF AUTHOR ▼

DATES OF BIRTH AND DEATH
Year Born ▼   Year Died ▼

Was this contribution to the work a
"work made for hire"?
☐ Yes
☐ No

AUTHOR'S NATIONALITY OR DOMICILE
Name of Country
OR { Citizen of _____
Domiciled in _____

WAS THIS AUTHOR'S CONTRIBUTION TO
THE WORK
Anonymous?   ☐ Yes ☐ No
Pseudonymous?   ☐ Yes ☐ No

If the answer to either
of these questions is
fiYes, see detailed
instructions.

NATURE OF AUTHORSHIP Briefly describe nature of material created by this author in which copyright is claimed. ▼

c
NAME OF AUTHOR ▼

DATES OF BIRTH AND DEATH
Year Born ▼   Year Died ▼

Was this contribution to the work a
"work made for hire"?
☐ Yes
☐ No

AUTHOR'S NATIONALITY OR DOMICILE
Name of Country
OR { Citizen of _____
Domiciled in _____

WAS THIS AUTHOR'S CONTRIBUTION TO
THE WORK
Anonymous?   ☐ Yes ☐ No
Pseudonymous?   ☐ Yes ☐ No

If the answer to either
of these questions is
fiYes, see detailed
instructions.

NATURE OF AUTHORSHIP Briefly describe nature of material created by this author in which copyright is claimed. ▼

3 a
YEAR IN WHICH CREATION OF THIS
WORK WAS COMPLETED   This information
must be given
_____ Year in all cases.

b
DATE AND NATION OF FIRST PUBLICATION OF THIS PARTICULAR WORK
Complete this information   Month _____ Day _____ Year _____
ONLY if this work
has been published.   Nation

4
COPYRIGHT CLAIMANT(S) Name and address must be given even if the claimant is the same as
the author given in space 2. ▼

See instructions
before completing
this space.

TRANSFER If the claimant(s) named here in space 4 is (are) different from the author(s) named in
space 2, give a brief statement of how the claimant(s) obtained ownership of the copyright. ▼

DO NOT WRITE HERE
OFFICE USE ONLY

APPLICATION RECEIVED

ONE DEPOSIT RECEIVED

TWO DEPOSITS RECEIVED

FUNDS RECEIVED

MORE ON BACK ▶   Complete all applicable spaces (numbers 5-9) on the reverse side of this page.
See detailed instructions.   Sign the form at line 8.

DO NOT WRITE HERE

Page 1 of _____ pages

Copyright
PA (Performing Arts)

EXAMINED BY	FORM PA
CHECKED BY	
☐ CORRESPONDENCE Yes	FOR COPYRIGHT OFFICE USE ONLY

DO NOT WRITE ABOVE THIS LINE. IF YOU NEED MORE SPACE, USE A SEPARATE CONTINUATION SHEET.

PREVIOUS REGISTRATION Has registration for this work, or for an earlier version of this work, already been made in the Copyright Office?

☐ **Yes** ☐ **No** If your answer is "Yes," why is another registration being sought? (Check appropriate box.) ▼ If your answer is No, do **not** check box A, B, or C.

a. ☐ This is the first published edition of a work previously registered in unpublished form.

b. ☐ This is the first application submitted by this author as copyright claimant.

c. ☐ This is a changed version of the work, as shown by space 6 on this application.

If your answer is "Yes," give: **Previous Registration Number** ▼   **Year of Registration** ▼

5

DERIVATIVE WORK OR COMPILATION Complete both space 6a and 6b for a derivative work; complete only 6b for a compilation.

Preexisting Material Identify any preexisting work or works that this work is based on or incorporates. ▼

a **6**

See instructions before completing this space.

Material Added to This Work Give a brief, general statement of the material that has been added to this work and in which copyright is claimed. ▼

b

DEPOSIT ACCOUNT If the registration fee is to be charged to a Deposit Account established in the Copyright Office, give name and number of Account.

Name ▼   **Account Number** ▼

a **7**

CORRESPONDENCE Give name and address to which correspondence about this application should be sent. Name/Address/Apt/City/State/ZIP ▼

b

Area code and daytime telephone number   (   )   Fax number   (   )

Email

CERTIFICATION* I, the undersigned, hereby certify that I am the

Check only one ▶ { ☐ author
☐ other copyright claimant
☐ owner of exclusive right(s)
☐ authorized agent of _____
Name of author or other copyright claimant, or owner of exclusive right(s) ▲

of the work identified in this application and that the statements made by me in this application are correct to the best of my knowledge.

8

Typed or printed name and date ▼ If this application gives a date of publication in space 3, do not sign and submit it before that date.

                             Date

Handwritten signature (X) ▼

☞   x _____

Certificate will be mailed in window envelope to this address:	Name ▼	**YOU MUST:** Complete all necessary spaces Sign your application in space 8	**9**
	Number/Street/Apt ▼	**SEND ALL 3 ELEMENTS IN THE SAME PACKAGE:** 1. Application form 2. Nonrefundable filing fee in check or money order payable to *Register of Copyrights* 3. Deposit material	Fees are subject to change. For current fees, check the Copyright Office website at www.copyright.gov, write the Copyright Office, or call (202) 707-3000.
	City/State/ZIP ▼	**MAIL TO:** Library of Congress Copyright Office 101 Independence Avenue, S.E. Washington, D.C. 20559-6000	

*17 U.S.C. § 506(e): Any person who knowingly makes a false representation of a material fact in the application for copyright registration provided for by section 409, or in any written statement filed in connection with the application, shall be fined not more than $2,500.

Rev: June 2002 20,000   Web Rev: June 2002   ⊕ Printed on recycled paper   U.S. Government Printing Office: 2000-461-113/20,021

Copyright
PA Short Form

Copyright Office fees are subject to change. For current fees, check the Copyright Office website at *www.copyright.gov*, write the Copyright Office, or call (202) 707-3000.

C **Short Form PA**
For a Work of Performing Arts
UNITED STATES COPYRIGHT OFFICE

REGISTRATION NUMBER

PA   PAU

Effective Date of Registration

Application Received

Examined By

Deposit Received
One   Two

Correspondence ☐   Fee Received

TYPE OR PRINT IN BLACK INK. DO NOT WRITE ABOVE THIS LINE.

Title of This Work: Alternative title or title of larger work in which this work was published:	**1**	
Name and Address of Author and Owner of the Copyright: Nationality or domicile: Phone, fax, and email:	**2**	Phone ( ) Fax ( ) Email:
Year of Creation:	**3**	
If work has been published, Date and Nation of Publication:	**4**	a. Date _____ _____ _____ *(Month, day, and* Month Day Year *year all required)* b. Nation
Type of Authorship in This Work: Check all that this author created.	**5**	☐ Music ☐ Other text (includes dramas, screenplays, etc.) ☐ Lyrics *(If your work is a motion picture or other audiovisual work, use the Standard Form PA.)*
Signature: (Registration cannot be completed without a signature.)	**6**	*I certify that the statements made by me in this application are correct to the best of my knowledge.** Check one: ☐ Author ☐ Authorized agent **X** _____
OPTIONAL **Name and Address of Person to Contact for Rights and Permissions:** Phone, fax, and email:	**7**	☐ Check here if same as #2 above. Phone ( ) Fax ( ) Email:

8

Certificate will be mailed in window envelope to this address:

Name ▼

Number/Street/Apt ▼

City/State/ZIP ▼

Complete this space only if you currently hold a Deposit Account in the Copyright Office.

9 Deposit Account # _____

Name _____

DO NOT WRITE HERE   Page 1 of _____ pages

*17 U.S.C. § 506(e): Any person who knowingly makes a false representation of a material fact in the application for copyright registration provided for by section 409, or in any written statement filed in connection with the application, shall be fined not more than $2,500.

Rev: July 2003—20,000   Web Rev: July 2003   ♻ Printed on recycled paper

U.S. Government Printing Office: 2003-496-605/60,025

127

Copyright Office fees are subject to change. For current fees, check the Copyright Office website at *www.copyright.gov*, write the Copyright Office, or call (202) 707-3000.

FORM SE
For a Serial
UNITED STATES COPYRIGHT OFFICE

REGISTRATION NUMBER

_____ U

EFFECTIVE DATE OF REGISTRATION

Month   Day   Year

DO NOT WRITE ABOVE THIS LINE. IF YOU NEED MORE SPACE, USE A SEPARATE CONTINUATION SHEET.

1

TITLE OF THIS SERIAL ▼

Volume ▼	Number ▼	Date on Copies ▼	Frequency of Publication ▼

PREVIOUS OR ALTERNATIVE TITLES ▼

2 a

NAME OF AUTHOR ▼

DATES OF BIRTH AND DEATH
Year Born ▼   Year Died ▼

Was this contribution to the work a "work made for hire"?
☐ Yes
☐ No

AUTHOR'S NATIONALITY OR DOMICILE
Name of Country
OR { Citizen of ▶ _____
Domiciled in ▶ _____

WAS THIS AUTHOR'S CONTRIBUTION TO THE WORK
Anonymous?   ☐ Yes ☐ No
Pseudonymous?   ☐ Yes ☐ No

If the answer to either of these questions is fiYes, see detailed instructions.

NATURE OF AUTHORSHIP   Briefly describe nature of material created by this author in which copyright is claimed. ▼
☐ Collective Work   Other:

NOTE

Under the law, the fiauthor of a fiwork made for hire is generally the employer, not the employee (see instructions). For any part of this work that was fimade for hire check fiYes in the space provided, give the employer (or other person for whom the work was prepared) as fiAuthor of that part, and leave the space for dates of birth and death blank.

b

NAME OF AUTHOR ▼

DATES OF BIRTH AND DEATH
Year Born ▼   Year Died ▼

Was this contribution to the work a "work made for hire"?
☐ Yes
☐ No

AUTHOR'S NATIONALITY OR DOMICILE
Name of Country
OR { Citizen of ▶ _____
Domiciled in ▶ _____

WAS THIS AUTHOR'S CONTRIBUTION TO THE WORK
Anonymous?   ☐ Yes ☐ No
Pseudonymous?   ☐ Yes ☐ No

If the answer to either of these questions is fiYes, see detailed instructions.

NATURE OF AUTHORSHIP   Briefly describe nature of material created by this author in which copyright is claimed. ▼
☐ Collective Work   Other:

c

NAME OF AUTHOR ▼

DATES OF BIRTH AND DEATH
Year Born ▼   Year Died ▼

Was this contribution to the work a "work made for hire"?
☐ Yes
☐No

AUTHOR'S NATIONALITY OR DOMICILE
Name of Country
OR { Citizen of ▶ _____
Domiciled in ▶ _____

WAS THIS AUTHOR'S CONTRIBUTION TO THE WORK
Anonymous?   ☐ Yes ☐ No
Pseudonymous?   ☐ Yes ☐ No

If the answer to either of these questions is fiYes, see detailed instructions.

NATURE OF AUTHORSHIP   Briefly describe nature of material created by this author in which copyright is claimed. ▼
☐ Collective Work   Other:

3 a

YEAR IN WHICH CREATION OF THIS ISSUE WAS COMPLETED
This information must be given ◀ Year in all cases.

b

DATE AND NATION OF FIRST PUBLICATION OF THIS PARTICULAR ISSUE
Complete this information ONLY if this work has been published.
Month ▶ _____ Day ▶ _____ Year ▶ _____ ◀ Nation

4

See instructions before completing this space.

COPYRIGHT CLAIMANT(S) Name and address must be given even if the claimant is the same as the author given in space 2. ▼

TRANSFER If the claimant(s) named here in space 4 is (are) different from the author(s) named in space 2, give a brief statement of how the claimant(s) obtained ownership of the copyright. ▼

DO NOT WRITE HERE
OFFICE USE ONLY

APPLICATION RECEIVED

ONE DEPOSIT RECEIVED

TWO DEPOSITS RECEIVED

REMITTANCE NUMBER AND DATE

MORE ON BACK ▶   Complete all applicable spaces (numbers 5-11) on the reverse side of this page.
See detailed instructions.   Sign the form at line 10.

DO NOT WRITE HERE
Page 1 of _____ pages

128

EXAMINED BY	FORM SE
CHECKED BY	
☐ CORRESPONDENCE Yes	FOR COPYRIGHT OFFICE USE ONLY

DO NOT WRITE ABOVE THIS LINE. IF YOU NEED MORE SPACE, USE A SEPARATE CONTINUATION SHEET.

PREVIOUS REGISTRATION Has registration for this work, or for an earlier version of this work, already been made in the Copyright Office?
☐ Yes ☐ No If your answer is "Yes," why is another registration being sought? (Check appropriate box.) ▼
a. ☐ This is the first published edition of a work previously registered in unpublished form.
b. ☐ This is the first application submitted by this author as copyright claimant.
c. ☐ This is a changed version of the work, as shown by space 6 on this application.
If your answer is "Yes," give: **Previous Registration Number** ▼   **Year of Registration** ▼

5

DERIVATIVE WORK OR COMPILATION Complete both space 6a and 6b for a derivative work; complete only 6b for a compilation.
Preexisting Material Identify any preexisting work or works that this work is based on or incorporates. ▼

a

6

Material Added to This Work Give a brief, general statement of the material that has been added to this work and in which copyright is claimed. ▼

b

See instructions before completing this space.

DEPOSIT ACCOUNT If the registration fee is to be charged to a Deposit Account established in the Copyright Office, give name and number of Account.
Name ▼   **Account Number** ▼

a

7

CORRESPONDENCE Give name and address to which correspondence about this application should be sent.   Name/Address/Apt/City/State/ZIP ▼

b

Area code and daytime telephone number ▶   Fax number   ▶
Email ▶

CERTIFICATION* I, the undersigned, hereby certify that I am the
Check only one ▶
☐ author
☐ other copyright claimant
☐ owner of exclusive right(s)
☐ authorized agent of _____
of the work identified in this application and that the statements made by me in this application are correct to the best of my knowledge.
Name of author or other copyright claimant, or owner of exclusive right(s) ▲

8

Typed or printed name and date ▼ If this application gives a date of publication in space 3, do not sign and submit it before that date.

_____ Date ▶ _____

Handwritten signature (X) ▼

X _____

Certificate will be mailed in window envelope to this address:	Name ▼
	Number/Street/Apt ▼
	City/State/ZIP ▼

YOU MUST:
Complete all necessary spaces
Sign your application in space 8
SEND ALL 3 ELEMENTS IN THE SAME PACKAGE:
1. Application form
2. Nonrefundable filing fee in check or money order payable to *Register of Copyrights*
3. Deposit material
MAIL TO:
Library of Congress
Copyright Office
101 Independence Avenue, S.E.
Washington, D.C. 20559-6000

Fees are subject to change. For current fees, check the Copyright Office website at www.copyright.gov, write the Copyright Office, or call (202) 707-3000.

9

129

*17 U.S.C. § 506(e): Any person who knowingly makes a false representation of a material fact in the application for copyright registration provided for by section 409, or in any written statement filed in connection with the application, shall be fined not more than $2,500.

Rev: June 2002 20,000   Web Rev: June 2002   ♻ Printed on recycled paper   U.S. Government Printing Office: 2000-461-113/20,021

Copyright
SE (Short Form)

Copyright Office fees are subject to change. For current fees, check the Copyright Office website at *www.copyright.gov*, write the Copyright Office, or call (202) 707-3000.

Short Form SE
For a Serial
UNITED STATES COPYRIGHT OFFICE

REGISTRATION NUMBER

Effective Date of Registration

Examined By

Application Received

Correspondence ☐

Deposit Received
One | Two

Fee Received

DO NOT WRITE ABOVE THIS LINE.

1 TITLE OF THIS SERIAL AS IT APPEARS ON THE COPY

Volume▼   Number▼   Date on copies▼   ISSN▼

2 NAME AND ADDRESS OF THE AUTHOR AND COPYRIGHT CLAIMANT IN THIS COLLECTIVE WORK MADE FOR HIRE

3 DATE OF PUBLICATION OF THIS PARTICULAR ISSUE
Month ▼   Day ▼   Year ▼

YEAR IN WHICH CREATION OF THIS ISSUE WAS COMPLETED (IF EARLIER THAN THE YEAR OF PUBLICATION):

Year ▶

CERTIFICATION*: I, the undersigned, hereby certify that I am the copyright claimant or the authorized agent of the copyright claimant of the work identified in this application, that all the conditions specified in the instructions on the back of this form are met, that the statements made by me in this application are correct to the best of my knowledge.

Handwritten signature (X) _____

Typed or printed name of signer _____

PERSON TO CONTACT FOR CORRESPONDENCE ABOUT THIS CLAIM
Name ▶
Address (if other than given below) ▶ _____
Daytime phone ▶ ( )
Fax ▶ ( )   Email ▶

DEPOSIT ACCOUNT
Account number ▶ _____
Name of account ▶ _____

Certificate will be mailed in window envelope to this address:

Name▼

Number/Street/Apt ▼

City/State/ZIP▼

YOU MUST:
• Complete all necessary spaces
• Sign your application
SEND ALL 3 ELEMENTS IN THE SAME PACKAGE:
1. Application form
2. Nonrefundable $30 filing fee in check or money order payable to *Register of Copyrights*
3. Deposit material
MAIL TO:
Library of Congress
Copyright Office
101 Independence Avenue, S.E.
Washington, D.C. 20559-6000

Fees are subject to change. For current fees, check the Copyright Office website at www.copyright.gov, write the Copyright Office, or call (202) 707-3000.

*17 U.S.C. §506(e): Any person who knowingly makes a false representation of a material fact in the application for copyright registration provided for by section 409, or in any written statement filed in connection with the application, shall be fined not more than $2,500.

Rev: June 2002—20,000   Web Rev: June 2002   ♲ Printed on recycled paper

U.S. Government Printing Office: 2000-461-113/20,021

130

Copyright Office fees are subject to change. For current fees, check the Copyright Office website at *www.copyright.gov*, write the Copyright Office, or call (202) 707-3000.

Form SE/Group
UNITED STATES COPYRIGHT OFFICE

REGISTRATION NUMBER

EFFECTIVE DATE OF REGISTRATION

APPLICATION RECEIVED

ONE DEPOSIT RECEIVED

EXAMINED BY   CORRESPONDENCE ☐

DO NOT WRITE ABOVE THIS LINE.

1

List in order of publication

No previous registration under **identical title** ☐

TITLE ▼   ISSN ▼

	Volume ▼	Number ▼	Issue date on copies ▼	Month, day, and year of publication ▼
1.				
2.				
3.				
4.				
5.				
6.				
7.				
8.				
9.				
10.				
11.				
12.				
13.				
14.				

2

NAME AND ADDRESS OF THE AUTHOR/COPYRIGHT CLAIMANT IN THESE COLLECTIVE WORKS MADE FOR HIRE ▼

FOR NON-U.S. WORKS: Author's citizenship ▼   Domicile ▼   Nation of publication ▼

CERTIFICATION*:   I, the undersigned, hereby certify that I am the copyright claimant or the authorized agent of the copyright claimant of the works identified in this application, that all the conditions specified in the instructions on the back of this form are met, that I have deposited two complimentary subscription copies with the Library of Congress, and that the statements made by me in this application are correct to the best of my knowledge.

Handwritten signature (X) _____   Typed or printed name _____

PERSON TO CONTACT FOR CORRESPONDENCE ABOUT THIS CLAIM
Name _____   Daytime telephone _____
Address (if other than given below) _____

Fax _____   Email _____

Certificate will be mailed in window envelope to this address:

Name ▼

Number/Street/Apt ▼

City/State/ZIP ▼

DEPOSIT ACCOUNT
Account number _____
Name of account _____

MAIL TO:
Library of Congress
Copyright Office
101 Independence Avenue, S.E.
Washington, D.C. 20559-6000

*17 U.S.C. §506(e): Any person who knowingly makes a false representation of a material fact in the application for copyright registration provided for by section 409, or in any written statement filed in connection with the application, shall be fined not more than $2,500.

Rev: July 2002—70,000   Web Rev: July 2002   Printed on recycled paper   U.S. Government Printing Office: 2003-496-605/60,019

Copyright
SE/Group/Daily Newspapers

Copyright Office fees are subject to change. For current fees, check the Copyright Office website at *www.copyright.gov*, write the Copyright Office, or call (202) 707-3000.

Ⓒ Form G/DN
For Group/Daily Newspapers and Newsletters
UNITED STATES COPYRIGHT OFFICE

REGISTRATION NUMBER

EFFECTIVE DATE OF REGISTRATION
(Assigned by Copyright Office)

Month	Day	Year

APPLICATION RECEIVED

EXAMINED BY

ONE DEPOSIT RECEIVED

CORRESPONDENCE ☐

FEE RECEIVED

DO NOT WRITE ABOVE THIS LINE.

1 TITLE OF THIS ☐ NEWSPAPER AS IT APPEARS ON THE COPIES ▼   City / State▼
☐ NEWSLETTER

If no previous registration under identical title, check here ☐

Month and year date on copies ▼   Number of issues in this group ▼   ISSN▼   Edition▼

2 NAME AND ADDRESS OF THE AUTHOR/COPYRIGHT CLAIMANT IN THESE WORKS MADE FOR HIRE

AUTHOR'S CONTRIBUTION (check all that apply)

☐ Editing   ☐ Compilation   ☐ Text   ☐ Other_____

3 DATE OF PUBLICATION OF THE FIRST AND LAST ISSUES IN THIS GROUP   Important: Give month, day, and year

(First) _____   (Last) _____
Month ▲   Day▲   Year▲   Month ▲   Day▲   Year▲

CERTIFICATION*:   I, the undersigned, hereby certify that I am the copyright claimant or the authorized agent of the copyright claimant of the works identified in this application, that all the conditions specified in the instructions on the back of this form are met, and that the statements made by me in this application are correct to the best of my knowledge.

Handwritten
signature (X) _____

Typed or printed
name of signer _____

PERSON TO CONTACT FOR CORRESPONDENCE ABOUT THIS CLAIM

Name _____
Daytime telephone number ( ) _____
Address (if other than given below) _____

Fax _____   Email _____

DEPOSIT ACCOUNT
Account number _____
Name of account _____

Certificate will be mailed in window envelope to this address

Name▼

Number/Street/Apt ▼

City/State/ZIP▼

YOU MUST:
• Complete all necessary spaces
• Sign your application
SEND ALL 3 ELEMENTS IN THE SAME PACKAGE:
1. Application form
2. Nonrefundable filing fee in check or money order payable to *Register of Copyrights*
3. Deposit material
MAIL TO:
Library of Congress, Copyright Office
101 Independence Avenue, S.E.
Washington, D.C. 20559-6000

Fees are subject to change. For current fees, check the Copyright Office website at www.copyright.gov, write the Copyright Office, or call (202) 707-3000.

*17 U.S.C. §506(e): Any person who knowingly makes a false representation of a material fact in the application for copyright registration provided for by section 409, or in any written statement filed in connection with the application, shall be fined not more than $2,500.

Rev: June 2002—20,000   Web Rev: June 2002   Ⓖ Printed on recycled paper

U.S. Government Printing Office: 2000-461-113/20,021

Copyright Office fees are subject to change. For current fees, check the Copyright Office website at *www.copyright.gov*, write the Copyright Office, or call (202) 707-3000.

Ⓒ Form SR
For a Sound Recording
UNITED STATES COPYRIGHT OFFICE

REGISTRATION NUMBER

_____

SR   SRU

EFFECTIVE DATE OF REGISTRATION

_____

Month   Day   Year

DO NOT WRITE ABOVE THIS LINE. IF YOU NEED MORE SPACE, USE A SEPARATE CONTINUATION SHEET.

1 TITLE OF THIS WORK ▼

PREVIOUS, ALTERNATIVE, OR CONTENTS TITLES (CIRCLE ONE) ▼

2 **a** NAME OF AUTHOR ▼

DATES OF BIRTH AND DEATH
Year Born ▼   Year Died ▼

Was this contribution to the work a "work made for hire"?
☐ Yes
☐ No

AUTHOR'S NATIONALITY OR DOMICILE
Name of Country
OR { Citizen of ▶ _____
      Domiciled in ▶ _____

WAS THIS AUTHOR'S CONTRIBUTION TO THE WORK
Anonymous?   ☐ Yes ☐ No
Pseudonymous? ☐ Yes ☐ No

If the answer to either of these questions is "Yes," see detailed instructions.

NATURE OF AUTHORSHIP Briefly describe nature of material created by this author in which copyright is claimed. ▼

NOTE

Under the law, the "author" of a "work made for hire" is generally the employer, not the employee (see instructions). For any part of this work that was "made for hire," check "Yes" in the space provided, give the employer (or other person for whom the work was prepared) as "Author" of that part, and leave the space for dates of birth and death blank.

b NAME OF AUTHOR ▼

DATES OF BIRTH AND DEATH
Year Born ▼   Year Died ▼

Was this contribution to the work a "work made for hire"?
☐ Yes
☐ No

AUTHOR'S NATIONALITY OR DOMICILE
Name of Country
OR { Citizen of ▶ _____
      Domiciled in ▶ _____

WAS THIS AUTHOR'S CONTRIBUTION TO THE WORK
Anonymous?   ☐ Yes ☐ No
Pseudonymous? ☐ Yes ☐ No

If the answer to either of these questions is "Yes," see detailed instructions.

NATURE OF AUTHORSHIP Briefly describe nature of material created by this author in which copyright is claimed. ▼

c NAME OF AUTHOR ▼

DATES OF BIRTH AND DEATH
Year Born ▼   Year Died ▼

Was this contribution to the work a "work made for hire"?
☐ Yes
☐ No

AUTHOR'S NATIONALITY OR DOMICILE
Name of Country
OR { Citizen of ▶ _____
      Domiciled in ▶ _____

WAS THIS AUTHOR'S CONTRIBUTION TO THE WORK
Anonymous?   ☐ Yes ☐ No
Pseudonymous? ☐ Yes ☐ No

If the answer to either of these questions is "Yes," see detailed instructions.

NATURE OF AUTHORSHIP Briefly describe nature of material created by this author in which copyright is claimed. ▼

3 **a** YEAR IN WHICH CREATION OF THIS WORK WAS COMPLETED
_____ ◀ Year This information must be given in all cases.

b DATE AND NATION OF FIRST PUBLICATION OF THIS PARTICULAR WORK
Complete this information ONLY if this work has been published.
Month ▶ _____ Day ▶ _____ Year ▶ _____
_____ ◀ Nation

4 **a** COPYRIGHT CLAIMANT(S) Name and address must be given even if the claimant is the same as the author given in space 2. ▼

See instructions before completing this space.

b TRANSFER If the claimant(s) named here in space 4 is (are) different from the author(s) named in space 2, give a brief statement of how the claimant(s) obtained ownership of the copyright. ▼

APPLICATION RECEIVED
_____

ONE DEPOSIT RECEIVED
_____

TWO DEPOSITS RECEIVED
_____

FUNDS RECEIVED

DO NOT WRITE HERE
OFFICE USE ONLY

MORE ON BACK ▶ • Complete all applicable spaces (numbers 5-9) on the reverse side of this page.
• See detailed instructions.   • Sign the form at line 8.

DO NOT WRITE HERE
Page 1 of _____ pages

133

Copyright
SR (Sound Recordings)

EXAMINED BY	FORM SR
CHECKED BY	
CORRESPONDENCE ❏ Yes	FOR COPYRIGHT OFFICE USE ONLY

DO NOT WRITE ABOVE THIS LINE. IF YOU NEED MORE SPACE, USE A SEPARATE CONTINUATION SHEET.

PREVIOUS REGISTRATION Has registration for this work, or for an earlier version of this work, already been made in the Copyright Office?

❏ Yes ❏ No If your answer is "Yes," why is another registration being sought? (Check appropriate box) ▼

a. ❏ This work was previously registered in unpublished form and now has been published for the first time.

b. ❏ This is the first application submitted by this author as copyright claimant.

c. ❏ This is a changed version of the work, as shown by space 6 on this application.

If your answer is "Yes," give: **Previous Registration Number** ▼   **Year of Registration** ▼

5

DERIVATIVE WORK OR COMPILATION
Preexisting Material Identify any preexisting work or works that this work is based on or incorporates. ▼

a

Material Added to This Work Give a brief, general statement of the material that has been added to this work and in which copyright is claimed. ▼

b

6

See instructions before completing this space.

DEPOSIT ACCOUNT If the registration fee is to be charged to a Deposit Account established in the Copyright Office, give name and number of Account.
    Name ▼   Account Number ▼

a

CORRESPONDENCE Give name and address to which correspondence about this application should be sent.   Name/Address/Apt/City/State/ZIP ▼

b

Area code and daytime telephone number   Fax number
Email

7

CERTIFICATION* I, the undersigned, hereby certify that I am the

Check only one ▼

❏ author

❏ other copyright claimant

❏ owner of exclusive right(s)

❏ authorized agent of _____
              Name of author or other copyright claimant, or owner of exclusive right(s) ▲

of the work identified in this application and that the statements made by me in this application are correct to the best of my knowledge.

Typed or printed name and date ▼ If this application gives a date of publication in space 3, do not sign and submit it before that date.

    Date _____

Handwritten signature (x) ▼

X _

8

Certificate will be mailed in window envelope to this address	Name ▼ Number/Street/Apt ▼ City/State/ZIP ▼

YOU MUST:
• Complete all necessary spaces
• Sign your application in space 8

SEND ALL 3 ELEMENTS IN THE SAME PACKAGE:
1. Application form
2. Nonrefundable filing fee in check or money order payable to *Register of Copyrights*
3. Deposit material

MAIL TO:
Library of Congress
Copyright Office - SR
101 Independence Avenue, S.E.
Washington, D.C. 20559-6237

Fees are subject to change. For current fees, check the Copyright Office website at www.copyright.gov, write the Copyright Office, or call (202) 707-3000.

9

*17 U.S.C. § 506(e): Any person who knowingly makes a false representation of a material fact in the application for copyright registration provided for by section 409, or in any written statement filed in connection with the application, shall be fined not more than $2,500.

Rev: July 2003—100,000   Web Rev: July 2003   ♲ Printed on recycled paper   U.S. Government Printing Office: 2003-496-605/60,0xx

Copyright Office fees are subject to change. For current fees, check the Copyright Office website at *www.copyright.gov*, write the Copyright Office, or call (202) 707-3000.

Form VA
For a Work of the Visual Arts
UNITED STATES COPYRIGHT OFFICE

REGISTRATION NUMBER

VA   VAU

EFFECTIVE DATE OF REGISTRATION

Month   Day   Year

DO NOT WRITE ABOVE THIS LINE. IF YOU NEED MORE SPACE, USE A SEPARATE CONTINUATION SHEET.

1

Title of This Work ▼   NATURE OF THIS WORK ▼ See instructions

Previous or Alternative Titles ▼

Publication as a Contribution If this work was published as a contribution to a periodical, serial, or collection, give information about the collective work in which the contribution appeared. **Title of Collective Work** ▼

If published in a periodical or serial give: Volume ▼   Number ▼   Issue Date ▼   On Pages ▼

2

a

NAME OF AUTHOR ▼   DATES OF BIRTH AND DEATH
Year Born ▼   Year Died ▼

NOTE

Under the law, the "author" of a **"work made for hire"** is generally the employer, not the employee (see instructions). For any part of this work that was "made for hire" check "Yes" in the space provided, give the employer (or other person for whom the work was prepared) as "Author" of that part, and leave the space for dates of birth and death blank.

Was this contribution to the work a "work made for hire"?
☐ Yes
☐ No

Author's Nationality or Domicile
Name of Country
OR { Citizen of _____
Domiciled in _____

Was This Author's Contribution to the Work
Anonymous? ☐ Yes ☐ No
Pseudonymous? ☐ Yes ☐ No

If the answer to either of these questions is "Yes," see detailed instructions.

Nature of Authorship Check appropriate box(es). **See instructions**
☐ 3-Dimensional sculpture   ☐ Map   ☐ Technical drawing
☐ 2-Dimensional artwork   ☐ Photograph   ☐ Text
☐ Reproduction of work of art ☐ Jewelry design ☐ Architectural work

b

Name of Author ▼   Dates of Birth and Death
Year Born ▼   Year Died ▼

Was this contribution to the work a "work made for hire"?
☐ Yes
☐ No

Author's Nationality or Domicile
Name of Country
OR { Citizen of _____
Domiciled in _____

Was This Author's Contribution to the Work
Anonymous? ☐ Yes ☐ No
Pseudonymous? ☐ Yes ☐ No

If the answer to either of these questions is "Yes," see detailed instructions.

Nature of Authorship Check appropriate box(es). **See instructions**
☐ 3-Dimensional sculpture   ☐ Map   ☐ Technical drawing
☐ 2-Dimensional artwork   ☐ Photograph   ☐ Text
☐ Reproduction of work of art ☐ Jewelry design ☐ Architectural work

3

a Year in Which Creation of This Work Was Completed
_____ Year
This information must be given in all cases.

b Date and Nation of First Publication of This Particular Work
Complete this information ONLY if this work has been published.
Month _____ Day _____ Year _____
_____ Nation

4

See instructions before completing this space.

COPYRIGHT CLAIMANT(S) Name and address must be given even if the claimant is the same as the author given in space 2. ▼

Transfer If the claimant(s) named here in space 4 is (are) different from the author(s) named in space 2, give a brief statement of how the claimant(s) obtained ownership of the copyright. ▼

DO NOT WRITE HERE
OFFICE USE ONLY

APPLICATION RECEIVED

ONE DEPOSIT RECEIVED

TWO DEPOSITS RECEIVED

FUNDS RECEIVED

MORE ON BACK ▶ • Complete all applicable spaces (numbers 5-9) on the reverse side of this page.
• See detailed instructions. • Sign the form at line 8.

DO NOT WRITE HERE
Page 1 of _____ pages

Copyright
VA (Visual Arts)

EXAMINED BY _____	FORM VA
CHECKED BY _____	
☐ CORRESPONDENCE Yes	FOR COPYRIGHT OFFICE USE ONLY

DO NOT WRITE ABOVE THIS LINE. IF YOU NEED MORE SPACE, USE A SEPARATE CONTINUATION SHEET.

PREVIOUS REGISTRATION Has registration for this work, or for an earlier version of this work, already been made in the Copyright Office?

☐ **Yes** ☐ **No** If your answer is "Yes," why is another registration being sought? (Check appropriate box.) ▼

a. ☐ This is the first published edition of a work previously registered in unpublished form.

b. ☐ This is the first application submitted by this author as copyright claimant.

c. ☐ This is a changed version of the work, as shown by space 6 on this application.

If your answer is "Yes," give: **Previous Registration Number** ▼   **Year of Registration** ▼

5

DERIVATIVE WORK OR COMPILATION Complete both space 6a and 6b for a derivative work; complete only 6b for a compilation.

a. Preexisting Material Identify any preexisting work or works that this work is based on or incorporates. ▼

b. Material Added to This Work Give a brief, general statement of the material that has been added to this work and in which copyright is claimed. ▼

6
a
b
See instructions before completing this space.

DEPOSIT ACCOUNT If the registration fee is to be charged to a Deposit Account established in the Copyright Office, give name and number of Account.

Name ▼   **Account Number** ▼

CORRESPONDENCE Give name and address to which correspondence about this application should be sent. Name/Address/Apt/City/State/ZIP ▼

7
a
b

Area code and daytime telephone number   (   )   Fax number   (   )

Email

CERTIFICATION* I, the undersigned, hereby certify that I am the

check only one ▶ {
☐ author
☐ other copyright claimant
☐ owner of exclusive right(s)
☐ authorized agent of _____
Name of author or other copyright claimant, or owner of exclusive right(s) ▲

of the work identified in this application and that the statements made by me in this application are correct to the best of my knowledge.

8

Typed or printed name and date ▼ If this application gives a date of publication in space 3, do not sign and submit it before that date.

_____   Date _____

Handwritten signature (X) ▼

X _____

9

Certificate will be mailed in window envelope to this address:	**Name** ▼ **Number/Street/Apt** ▼ **City/State/ZIP** ▼	**YOU MUST:** • Complete all necessary spaces • Sign your application in space 8 **SEND ALL 3 ELEMENTS IN THE SAME PACKAGE:** 1. Application form 2. Nonrefundable filing fee in check or money order payable to *Register of Copyrights* 3. Deposit material **MAIL TO:** Library of Congress Copyright Office 101 Independence Avenue, S.E. Washington, D.C. 20559-6000

Fees are subject to change. For current fees, check the Copyright Office website at www.copyright.gov, write the Copyright Office, or call (202) 707-3000.

*17 U.S.C. § 506(e): Any person who knowingly makes a false representation of a material fact in the application for copyright registration provided for by section 409, or in any written statement filed in connection with the application, shall be fined not more than $2,500.

Rev: August 2003—30,000   Web Rev: June 2002   ♻ Printed on recycled paper   U.S. Government Printing Office: 2003-496-605/60,029

Copyright Office fees are subject to change.
For current fees, check the Copyright Office
website at *www.copyright.gov*, write the Copyright Office, or call (202) 707-3000.

C Short Form VA
For a Work of the Visual Arts
UNITED STATES COPYRIGHT OFFICE

REGISTRATION NUMBER

| VA | VAU |

Effective Date of Registration

Application Received

Examined By

Deposit Received
One   Two

Correspondence ☐

Fee Received

TYPE OR PRINT IN BLACK INK. DO NOT WRITE ABOVE THIS LINE.

1 Title of This Work:

Alternative title or title of
larger work in which this
work was published:

**2 Name and Address of
Author and Owner of the
Copyright:**

Nationality or domicile:
Phone, fax, and email:

Phone (   )   Fax (   )
Email

3 Year of Creation:

**4 If work has been published,
Date and Nation of
Publication:**

a. Date _____ _____ _____ *(Month, day, and*
                 Month   Day   Year   *year all required)*

b. Nation

**5 Type of Authorship
in This Work:**
Check all that this author created.

☐ 3-Dimensional sculpture   ☐ Photograph   ☐ Map
☐ 2-Dimensional artwork   ☐ Jewelry design ☐ Text
☐ Technical drawing

6 Signature:

Registration cannot be
completed without a signature.

I certify that the statements made by me in this application are correct to the best of my knowledge. * Check one:

☐ Author   ☐ Authorized agent

X _

**7 Name and Address of
Person to Contact for
Rights and Permissions:**
Phone, fax, and email:

OPTIONAL

☐ Check here if same as #2 above.

Phone (   )   Fax (   )
Email

8
Certificate
will be
mailed in
window
envelope to
this address:

Name ▼

Number/Street/Apt ▼

City/State/ZIP ▼

Complete this space only
if you currently hold a
Deposit Account in
the Copyright
Office.

9 Deposit Account #_____

Name _____

_____

_____

DO NOT WRITE HERE   Page 1 of _____ pages

**17 U.S.C. § 506(e): Any person who knowingly makes a false representation of a material fact in the application for copyright registration provided for by section 409, or in any written statement filed in connection with
the application, shall be fined not more than $2,500.*

August 2003—30,000   Web Rev: August 2003   ♻ Printed on recycled paper

U.S. Government Printing Office: 2003-496-605/60,031

CONTINUATION SHEET FOR APPLICATION FORMS

Form _____ /CON
UNITED STATES COPYRIGHT OFFICE

REGISTRATION NUMBER

PA	PAU	SE	SEG	SEU	SR	SRU	TX	TXU	VA	VAU

EFFECTIVE DATE OF REGISTRATION

(Month)   (Day)   (Year)

CONTINUATION SHEET RECEIVED

- This Continuation Sheet is used in conjunction with Forms CA, PA, SE, SR, TX, and VA, **only**. Indicate which basic form you are continuing in the space in the upper right-hand corner.
- If at all possible, try to fit the information called for into the spaces provided on the basic form.
- If you do not have enough space for all the information you need to give on the basic form, use this Continuation Sheet and submit it with the basic form.
- If you submit this Continuation Sheet, clip (do not tape or staple) it to the basic form and fold the two together before submitting them.
- **Space A of this sheet is intended to identify the basic application.**
  Space B is a continuation of Space 2 on the basic application.
  Space B is not applicable to Short Forms.
  Space C (on the reverse side of this sheet) is for the continuation of Spaces 1, 4, or 6 on the basic application or for the continuation of Space 1 on any of the three Short Forms PA, TX, or VA.

Page _____ of _____ pages

DO NOT WRITE ABOVE THIS LINE. FOR COPYRIGHT OFFICE USE ONLY

A
Identification of Application

IDENTIFICATION OF CONTINUATION SHEET: This sheet is a continuation of the application for copyright registration on the basic form submitted for the following work:
- TITLE: (Give the title as given under the heading "Title of this Work" in Space 1 of the basic form.)

....

- NAME(S) AND ADDRESS(ES) OF COPYRIGHT CLAIMANT(S) : (Give the name and address of at least one copyright claimant as given in Space 4 of the basic form or Space 2 of any of the Short Forms PA, TX, or VA.)

B
Continuation of Space 2

d

NAME OF AUTHOR ▼

DATES OF BIRTH AND DEATH
Year Born▼   Year Died▼

Was this contribution to the work a "work made for hire"?
❑ Yes
❑ No

AUTHOR'S NATIONALITY OR DOMICILE
Name of Country
OR { Citizen of ▶ _____
     Domiciled in ▶ _____

WAS THIS AUTHOR'S CONTRIBUTION TO THE WORK
Anonymous? ❑ Yes ❑ No
Pseudonymous? ❑ Yes ❑ No
If the answer to either of these questions is "Yes," see detailed instructions.

NATURE OF AUTHORSHIP Briefly describe nature of the material created by the author in which copyright is claimed. ▼

e

NAME OF AUTHOR ▼

DATES OF BIRTH AND DEATH
Year Born▼   Year Died▼

Was this contribution to the work a "work made for hire"?
❑ Yes
❑ No

AUTHOR'S NATIONALITY OR DOMICILE
Name of Country
OR { Citizen of ▶ _____
     Domiciled in ▶ _____

WAS THIS AUTHOR'S CONTRIBUTION TO THE WORK
Anonymous? ❑ Yes ❑ No
Pseudonymous? ❑ Yes ❑ No
If the answer to either of these questions is "Yes," see detailed instructions.

NATURE OF AUTHORSHIP Briefly describe nature of the material created by the author in which copyright is claimed. ▼

f

NAME OF AUTHOR ▼

DATES OF BIRTH AND DEATH
Year Born▼   Year Died▼

Was this contribution to the work a "work made for hire"?
❑ Yes
❑ No

AUTHOR'S NATIONALITY OR DOMICILE
Name of Country
OR { Citizen of ▶ _____
     Domiciled in ▶ _____

WAS THIS AUTHOR'S CONTRIBUTION TO THE WORK
Anonymous? ❑ Yes ❑ No
Pseudonymous? ❑ Yes ❑ No
If the answer to either of these questions is "Yes," see detailed instructions.

NATURE OF AUTHORSHIP Briefly describe nature of the material created by the author in which copyright is claimed. ▼

Use the reverse side of this sheet if you need more space for continuation of Spaces 1, 4, or 6 of the basic form or for the continuation of Space 1 on any of the Short Forms PA, TX, or VA.

Copyright Office fees are subject to change. For current fees, check the Copyright Office website at *www.copyright.gov*, write the Copyright Office, or call (202) 707-3000.

Form CA
For Supplementary Registration
UNITED STATES COPYRIGHT OFFICE

REGISTRATION NUMBER

TX	TXU	PA	PAU	VA	VAU	SR	SRU	RE

EFFECTIVE DATE OF SUPPLEMENTARY REGISTRATION

Month   Day   Year

DO NOT WRITE ABOVE THIS LINE. IF YOU NEED MORE SPACE, USE A SEPARATE CONTINUATION SHEET.

A

Title of Work ▼

Registration Number of the Basic Registration ▼

Year of Basic Registration ▼

Name(s) of Author(s) ▼

Name(s) of Copyright Claimant(s) ▼

B

Location and Nature of Incorrect Information in Basic Registration ▼

Line Number _____ Line Heading or Description _____

Incorrect Information as It Appears in Basic Registration ▼

Corrected Information ▼

Explanation of Correction ▼

C

Location and Nature of Information in Basic Registration to be Amplified ▼

Line Number _____ Line Heading or Description _____

Amplified Information and Explanation of Information ▼

MORE ON BACK ▶ • Complete all applicable spaces (D-G) on the reverse side of this page.
• See detailed instructions.   • Sign the form at Space F.

DO NOT WRITE HERE

Page 1 of _____ pages

139

Copyright
CA (Corrections of Application)

FORM CA RECEIVED

FUNDS RECEIVED DATE

EXAMINED BY

CORRESPONDENCE ❑

REFERENCE TO THIS REGISTRATION ADDED TO
BASIC REGISTRATION ❑ YES ❑ NO

FORM CA

FOR
COPYRIGHT
OFFICE
USE
ONLY

DO NOT WRITE ABOVE THIS LINE. IF YOU NEED MORE SPACE, USE A SEPARATE CONTINUATION SHEET.

Continuation of: ❑ Part B *or* ❑ Part C

D

Correspondence: Give name and address to which correspondence about this application should be sent.

E

Phone (____)_____ Fax (____)_____ Email _____

Deposit Account: If the registration fee is to be charged to a Deposit Account established in the Copyright Office, give name and number of Account.

Name _____

Account Number _____

Certification* I, the undersigned, hereby certify that I am the: (Check only one)
❑ author ❑ owner of exclusive right(s)
❑ other copyright claimant ❑ duly authorized agent of _____
Name of author or other copyright claimant, or owner of exclusive right(s) ▲
of the work identified in this application and that the statements made by me in this application are correct to the best of my knowledge.

F

Typed or printed name ▼ _____ **Date ▼** _____

Handwritten signature (X) ▼

Certificate will be mailed in window envelope to this address:

Name ▼

Number/Street/Apt ▼

City/State/ZIP ▼

YOU MUST:
• Complete all necessary spaces
• Sign your application in Space F
SEND ALL ELEMENTS IN THE SAME PACKAGE:
1. Application form
2. Nonrefundable filing fee in check or money order payable to *Register of Copyrights*
MAIL TO:
Library of Congress
Copyright Office
101 Independence Avenue, S.E.
Washington, D.C. 20559-6000

Fees are subject to change. For current fees, check the Copyright Office website at www.copyright.gov, write the Copyright Office, or call (202) 707-3000.

G

*17 U.S.C. § 506(e): Any person who knowingly makes a false representation of a material fact in the application for copyright registration provided for by section 409, or in any written statement filed in connection with the application, shall be fined not more than $2,500.

Rev: July 2002—20,000 Web Rev: July 2002 Printed on recycled paper

U.S. Government Printing Office: 2002-491-423/60,009

Copyright Office fees are subject to change. For current fees, check the Copyright Office website at *www.copyright.gov*, write the Copyright Office, or call (202) 707-3000.

C **Form RE**
For Renewal of a Work
UNITED STATES COPYRIGHT OFFICE

REGISTRATION NUMBER

EFFECTIVE DATE OF RENEWAL REGISTRATION

Month   Day   Year

DO NOT WRITE ABOVE THIS LINE. IF YOU NEED MORE SPACE, USE A SEPARATE CONTINUATION SHEET (FORM RE/CON).

1

RENEWAL CLAIMANT(S), ADDRESS(ES), AND STATEMENT OF CLAIM ▼ (See Instructions)

a
Name ....
Address ....
Claiming as ....
(Use appropriate statement from instructions)

b
Name ....
Address ....
Claiming as ....

c
Name ....
Address ....
Claiming as ....

2

TITLE OF WORK IN WHICH RENEWAL IS CLAIMED ▼

RENEWABLE MATTER ▼

PUBLICATION AS A CONTRIBUTION If this work was published as a contribution to a periodical, serial, or other composite work, give information about the collective work in which the contribution appeared. **Title of Collective Work ▼**

If published in a periodical or serial, give: **Volume ▼**   **Number ▼**   **Issue Date ▼**

3

AUTHOR(S) OF RENEWABLE MATTER ▼ (If any author is deceased, give month, day, and year of death.)

Name: _____   Date of death: _____
Name: _____   Date of death: _____
Name: _____   Date of death: _____

4

ORIGINAL REGISTRATION NUMBER ▼   ORIGINAL COPYRIGHT CLAIMANT ▼

ORIGINAL DATE OF COPYRIGHT
If the original registration for this work was made in published form, give:
DATE OF PUBLICATION: _____
(Month)   (Day)   (Year)

OR

If the original registration for this work was made in unpublished form, give:
DATE OF REGISTRATION: _____
(Month)   (Day)   (Year)

MORE ON BACK ➤ • Complete all applicable spaces (numbers 5–8) on the reverse side of this page.
• See detailed instructions.   • Sign the form at space 7.

DO NOT WRITE HERE
Page 1 of _____ pages

Copyright
RE (Renewal)

RENEWAL APPLICATION RECEIVED	FORM RE
CORRESPONDENCE ❏ YES	
EXAMINED BY	FOR
CHECKED BY	COPYRIGHT OFFICE
FUNDS RECEIVED	USE ONLY

DO NOT WRITE ABOVE THIS LINE. IF YOU NEED MORE SPACE, USE A SEPARATE CONTINUATION SHEET (FORM RE/CON).

5

RENEWAL FOR GROUP OF WORKS BY SAME AUTHOR: To make a single registration for a group of works by the same individual author published as contributions to periodicals (see instructions), give full information about each contribution. If more space is needed, request continuation sheet (Form RE/CON).

a
Title of Contribution: ....
Title of Periodical: ....   Vol: .... No: .... Issue Date:.........
Date of Publication: ....   Registration Number: ....
(Month)   (Day)   (Year)

b
Title of Contribution: ....
Title of Periodical: ....   Vol: .... No: .... Issue Date:.........
Date of Publication: ....   Registration Number: ....
(Month)   (Day)   (Year)

c
Title of Contribution: ....
Title of Periodical: ....   Vol: .... No: .... Issue Date:.........
Date of Publication: ....   Registration Number: ....
(Month)   (Day)   (Year)

d
Title of Contribution: ....
Title of Periodical: ....   Vol: .... No: .... Issue Date:.........
Date of Publication: ....   Registration Number: ....
(Month)   (Day)   (Year)

6

DEPOSIT ACCOUNT: If the registration fee is to be charged to a Deposit Account established in the Copyright Office, give name and number of Account.

Name _____

_____

Account Number _____

Area code and daytime telephone number ▶ _____   Fax number ▶ _____

CORRESPONDENCE: Give name and address to which correspondence about this application should be sent.

Name _____

Address _____ (Apt)

(City)   (State)   (ZIP)

Email address ▶ _____

7

CERTIFICATION* I, the undersigned, hereby certify that I am the: (Check one)
❏ renewal claimant   ❏ duly authorized agent of _____
(Name of renewal claimant) ▲
of the work identified in this application and that the statements made by me in this application are correct to the best of my knowledge.

Typed or printed name ▼   **Date ▼**

_____   _____

Handwritten signature (X) ▼

_____

8

Certificate will be mailed in window envelope to this address:

Name ▼

Number/Street/Apt ▼

City/State/ZIP ▼

YOU MUST:
• Complete all necessary spaces
• Sign your application in space 7
SEND ALL ELEMENTS IN THE SAME PACKAGE:
1. Application form
2. Nonrefundable filing fee in check or money order payable to *Register of Copyrights*
MAIL TO:
Library of Congress
Copyright Office
101 Independence Avenue, S.E.
Washington, D.C. 20559-6000

Fees are subject to change. For current fees, check the Copyright Office website at www.copyright.gov, write the Copyright Office, or call (202) 707-3000.

*17 U.S.C. § 506(e): Any person who knowingly makes a false representation of a material fact in the application for copyright registration provided for by section 409, or in any written statement filed in connection with the application, shall be fined not more than $2,500.

Rev: July 2002—70,000   Web Rev: July 2002   Printed on recycled paper   U.S. Government Printing Office: 2003-496-605/60,018

Ⓒ Copyright Office Fees

Effective as of July 1, 2002

Basic Registrations

Fee to accompany an application and deposit for registration of a claim to copyright

- $30 Form TX
- $30 Short Form TX
- $30 Form VA
- $30 Short Form VA
- $30 Form PA
- $30 Short Form PA
- $30 Form SE
- $30 Short Form SE
- $30 Form SR
- $30 Form GATT
- — Form GR/CP (*This form is an adjunct to Forms VA, PA, and TX. There is no additional charge.*)

Renewal Registrations

For works published or registered before January 1, 1978

- $60 Form RE
- $30 Addendum to Form RE

Group Registrations

Fee to register a group of related claims, where appropriate

- $15 Form SE/Group (serials) (*minimum: $45*) (*$/serial issue*)
- $55 Form G/DN (daily newspapers and newsletters)
- $15 Form GATT/GRP (restored works) (*minimum: $45*) (*$/restored work*)

Supplementary Registrations

Fee to register a correction or amplification to a completed registration

- $100 Form CA

Miscellaneous Registrations

- $140 Form D-VH (vessel hulls)
- $75 Form MW (mask works)

Special Services Related to Registration (Optional Services)

Special Handling for Registration of Qualified Copyright Claims

Fee to expedite processing of qualified claims

- $580 Special handling fee (*per claim*)
- $50 Additional fee for each (nonspecial handling) claim using the same deposit

Other Fees Associated with Registration

- $425 Full-term retention of published copyright deposit
- $60 Secure test processing (*$/hr*)

Appeal Fees (*For claims previously refused registration*)

- $200 First appeal
- $20 Additional claim in related group (*each*)
- $500 Second appeal
- $20 Additional claim in related group (*each*)

Other Copyright Service Fees

Recordation of Documents Relating to Copyrighted Works

Fee to make a public record of an assignment of rights or other document

- $80 Recordation of a document containing no more than one title
- $20 Additional titles (*per group of 10 titles*)
- $30 Recordation of NIE containing no more than one title
- $1 Additional titles (*each*)
- $330 Special handling of recordation of documents

Reference and Bibliography Reports on Copyrighted Works

Fee for searching copyright records and preparing an official report

- $75 Preparation of a report from official records (*$/hr*)
- $250 Surcharge for *expedited* Reference and Bibl. reports (*$/hr*)

Certification and Documents Services: Preparing Copies of Copyright Office Records

Fees for locating, retrieving, and reproducing Copyright Office records

- $80 Locating and/or retrieving Copyright Office records (*$/hr*)
- $30 Additional certificate of registration (*$/hr*)
- $80 Certification of Copyright Office records (*$/hr*)
- — Copying fee: variable depending on format and size
- $100 Locating and/or retrieving in-process materials (*$/hr*)

- $200 **Surcharge for *Expedited* Certification and Documents Services**

Fee of $200/hr for total time spent in fulfilling any or all of these services

- — Locating and/or retrieving in-process records
- — Additional certificate of registration
- — Certification of Copyright Office records
- — Copy of assignment or other recorded document
- — Copy of any other Copyright Office record

Miscellaneous Fees

- $10 Receipt for deposit without registration (*Section 407 deposit*)
- $30 Online Service Provider Designation
- $50 Notice to Libraries and Archives (*each additional title: $20*)
- $12 Notice of Intention to obtain compulsory license to make and distribute phonorecords

Copyright Office fees are subject to change. For current fees, check the Copyright Office website at *www.copyright.gov*, write the Copyright Office, or call (202) 707-3000.

143

Trademark/Service Mark Application   Page 1 of 2

PTO Form 1478 (Rev 9/98)
OMB Control #0651-0009 (Exp. 08/31/2004)

Trademark/Service Mark Application

* To the Commissioner for Trademarks *

\<DOCUMENT INFORMATION>
\<TRADEMARK/SERVICEMARK APPLICATION>
\<VERSION 1.22>

\<APPLICANT INFORMATION>
\<NAME>   John A. Jones
\<STREET>   1234 Market Street
\<CITY>   Anywhere
\<STATE>   MI
\<COUNTRY>   USA
\<ZIP/POSTAL CODE>   22222-3333
\<TELEPHONE NUMBER>   800-444-5555
\<FAX NUMBER>   800-444-5550
\<E-MAIL ADDRESS>   jjones@aol.com
\<AUTHORIZE E-MAIL COMMUNICATION>   Yes

\<APPLICANT ENTITY INFORMATION>
\<INDIVIDUAL: COUNTRY OF CITIZENSHIP>   USA

\<TRADEMARK/SERVICEMARK INFORMATION>

\<MARK>   JJPUB

\<TYPED FORM>   Yes
~ Applicant requests registration of the above-identified trademark/service mark in the United States Patent and Trademark Office on the Principal Register established by the Act of July 5, 1946 (15 U.S.C. §1051 et seq., as amended). ~

\<BASIS FOR FILING AND GOODS/SERVICES INFORMATION>
\<USE IN COMMERCE: SECTION 1(a)>   Yes
~ Applicant is using or is using through a related company the mark in commerce on or in connection with the below-identified goods/services. (15 U.S.C. §1051(a), as amended.). Applicant attaches one SPECIMEN for each class showing the mark as used in commerce on or in connection with any item in the class of listed goods and/or services. ~
\<SPECIMEN DESCRIPTION>   shipping label; book cover
\<INTERNATIONAL CLASS NUMBER>   016
\<LISTING OF GOODS AND/OR SERVICES>   a housemark on a series of fiction and nonfiction books on a variety of topics
\<FIRST USE ANYWHERE DATE>   02/09/1999
\<FIRST USE IN COMMERCE DATE>   06/01/1999

\<FEE INFORMATION>

Trademark/Service Mark Application

Page 2 of 2

<LAW OFFICE INFORMATION>
~ The USPTO is authorized to communicate with the applicant at the below e-mail address ~
<E-MAIL ADDRESS FOR CORRESPONDENCE>   info@jjjjpub.com

<SIGNATURE AND OTHER INFORMATION>
~ **PTO-Application Declaration**: The undersigned, being hereby warned that willful false statements and the like so made are punishable by fine or imprisonment, or both, under 18 U.S.C. §1001, and that such willful false statements may jeopardize the validity of the application or any resulting registration, declares that he/she is properly authorized to execute this application on behalf of the applicant; he/she believes the applicant to be the owner of the trademark/service mark sought to be registered, or, if the application is being filed under 15 U.S.C. §1051(b), he/she believes applicant to be entitled to use such mark in commerce; to the best of his/her knowledge and belief no other person, firm, corporation, or association has the right to use the mark in commerce, either in the identical form thereof or in such near resemblance thereto as to be likely, when used on or in connection with the goods/services of such other person, to cause confusion, or to cause mistake, or to deceive; and that all statements made of his/her own knowledge are true; and that all statements made on information and belief are believed to be true. ~

<SIGNATURE>_____ * please sign here*

<DATE>   _____
<NAME>   John A. Jones
<TITLE>   President

Trademark/Service Mark Application

Page 1 of 2

PTO Form 1478 (Rev 9/98)
OMB Control #0651-0009 (Exp. 08/31/2004)

Trademark/Service Mark Application

* To the Commissioner for Trademarks *

<DOCUMENT INFORMATION>
<TRADEMARK/SERVICEMARK APPLICATION>
<VERSION 1.22>

<APPLICANT INFORMATION>
<NAME> JJJJ Publishing, LLC
<STREET> 1234 Main Street
<CITY> Anywhere
<STATE> PA
<COUNTRY> USA
<ZIP/POSTAL CODE> 11111-2222
<TELEPHONE NUMBER> 800-123-4444
<FAX NUMBER> 800-123-4440
<E-MAIL ADDRESS> info@jjjjpub.com
<AUTHORIZE E-MAIL COMMUNICATION> Yes

<APPLICANT ENTITY INFORMATION>
<OTHER ENTITY TYPE: SPECIFIC NATURE OF ENTITY> Limited Liability Company
<STATE/COUNTRY UNDER WHICH ORGANIZED> USA

<TRADEMARK/SERVICEMARK INFORMATION>

<MARK> JJJJPUB

<TYPED FORM> Yes
~ Applicant requests registration of the above-identified trademark/service mark in the United States Patent and Trademark Office on the Principal Register established by the Act of July 5, 1946 (15 U.S.C. §1051 et seq., as amended). ~

<BASIS FOR FILING AND GOODS/SERVICES INFORMATION>
<INTENT TO USE: SECTION 1(b)> Yes
~ Applicant has a bona fide intention to use or use through a related company the mark in commerce on or in connection with the below-identified goods/services. (15 U.S.C. §1051(b), as amended.) ~
<INTERNATIONAL CLASS NUMBER> 016
<LISTING OF GOODS AND/OR SERVICES> A series of fiction and nonfiction books on a variety of topics.

<FEE INFORMATION>
<TOTAL FEES PAID> 325
<NUMBER OF CLASSES PAID> 1
<NUMBER OF CLASSES> 1

Trademark/Service Mark Application   Page 2 of 2

\<LAW OFFICE INFORMATION\>
~ The USPTO is authorized to communicate with the applicant at the below e-mail address ~
\<E-MAIL ADDRESS FOR CORRESPONDENCE\>   info@jjjjpub.com

\<SIGNATURE AND OTHER INFORMATION\>
~ **PTO-Application Declaration**: The undersigned, being hereby warned that willful false statements and the like so made are punishable by fine or imprisonment, or both, under 18 U.S.C. §1001, and that such willful false statements may jeopardize the validity of the application or any resulting registration, declares that he/she is properly authorized to execute this application on behalf of the applicant; he/she believes the applicant to be the owner of the trademark/service mark sought to be registered, or, if the application is being filed under 15 U.S.C. §1051(b), he/she believes applicant to be entitled to use such mark in commerce; to the best of his/her knowledge and belief no other person, firm, corporation, or association has the right to use the mark in commerce, either in the identical form thereof or in such near resemblance thereto as to be likely, when used on or in connection with the goods/services of such other person, to cause confusion, or to cause mistake, or to deceive; and that all statements made of his/her own knowledge are true; and that all statements made on information and belief are believed to be true. ~

\<SIGNATURE\>_____ * please sign here*

\<DATE\>   _____
\<NAME\>   John A. Jones
\<TITLE\>   President

The information collected on this form allows the PTO to determine whether a mark may be registered on the Principal or Supplemental register, and provides notice of an applicant's claim of ownership of the mark. Responses to the request for information are required to obtain the benefit of a registration on the Principal or Supplemental register. 15 U.S.C. §§1051 et seq. and 37 C.F.R. Part 2. All information collected will be made public. Gathering and providing the information will require an estimated 12 or 18 minutes (depending if the application is based on an intent to use the mark in commerce, use of the mark in commerce, or a foreign application or registration). Please direct comments on the time needed to complete this form, and/or suggestions for reducing this burden to the Chief Information Officer, U.S. Patent and Trademark Office, U.S. Department of Commerce, Washington D.C. 20231. Please note that the PTO may not conduct or sponsor a collection of information using a form that does not display a valid OMB control number.

Trademarks
Trademark Application – TEAS

~TRADEMARK/SERVICE MARK APPLICATION (15 U.S.C. §§ 1051, 1126(d)&(e))~

NOTE: The following form complies with the provisions of the Trademark Law Treaty Implementation Act (TLTIA) and the fee increase effective January 10, 2000.

BASIC INSTRUCTIONS

The following form is written in a "scannable" format that will enable the U.S. Patent and Trademark Office (USPTO) to scan paper filings and capture application data automatically using optical character recognition (OCR) technology. Information is to be entered next to identifying data tags, such as <DATE OF FIRST USE IN COMMERCE>. OCR software can be programmed to identify these tags, capture the corresponding data, and transmit this data to the appropriate data fields in the Trademark databases, largely bypassing manual data entry processes.

Please enter the requested information in the blank space that appears to the right of each tagged (< >) element. However, do not enter any information immediately after the section headers (the bolded wording appearing in all capital letters). If you need additional space, first, in the space provided on the form, enter "See attached." Then, please use a separate piece of paper on which you first list the data tag (e.g., <LISTING OF GOODS AND/OR SERVICES>), followed by the relevant information. Some of the information requested *must* be provided. Other information is either required only in certain circumstances, or provided only at your discretion. **Please consult the "Help" section following the form for detailed explanations as to what information should be entered in each blank space.**

To increase the effectiveness of the USPTO scanners, it is recommended that you use a typewriter to complete the form.

For additional information, please see the *Basic Facts about Trademarks* booklet, available at http://www.uspto.gov/web/offices/tac/doc/basic/, or by calling the Trademark Assistance Center, at 703-308-9000. You may also wish to file electronically, from http://www.uspto.gov/teas/index.html.

MAILING INFORMATION

Send the completed form, appropriate fee(s) (made payable to "The Commissioner of Patent and Trademarks"), and any other required materials to:

> Box New App
> Fee
> Assistant Commissioner for Trademarks
> 2900 Crystal Drive
> Arlington, VA 22202-3513

The filing fee for this application is $325.00 *per class* of goods and/or services. You must include at least $325.00 with this application; otherwise the papers and money will be returned to you. Once your application meets the minimum filing date requirements, this processing fee becomes **non-refundable**. This is true even if the USPTO does not issue a registration certificate for this mark.

You may also wish to include a self-addressed stamped postcard with your submission, on which you identify the mark and list each item being submitted (e.g., application, fee, specimen, etc.). We will return this postcard to you, stamped with your assigned serial number, to confirm receipt of your submission.

~TRADEMARK/SERVICE MARK APPLICATION (15 U.S.C. §§ 1051, 1126(d)&(e))~

~To the Assistant Commissioner for Trademarks~

<APPLICANT INFORMATION>

<Name>

<Street>

<City>

<State>

<Country>

<Zip/Postal Code>

<Telephone Number>

<Fax Number>

<e-mail Address>

<APPLICANT ENTITY INFORMATION>~*Select only ONE*~

<Individual: Country of Citizenship>

<Corporation: State/Country of Incorporation>

<Partnership: State/Country under which Organized>

 <Name(s) of General Partner(s) & Citizenship/Incorporation>

<Other Entity Type: Specific Nature of Entity>

<State/Country under which Organized>

<TRADEMARK/SERVICE MARK INFORMATION>

<Mark>

<Typed Form>~*Enter YES, if appropriate*~

~*DISPLAY THE MARK that you want to register on a separate piece of paper (even if simply a word(s)). Please see additional HELP instructions.*~

<BASIS FOR FILING AND GOODS/SERVICES INFORMATION>

<Use in Commerce: Section 1(a)>~*Applicant is using or is using through a related company the mark in commerce on or in connection with the below-identified goods and/or services (15 U.S.C § 1051(a)).*~

<International Class Number(s)>

<Listing of Goods and/or Services>~*List in ascending numerical class order. Please see sample in HELP instructions.*~

<Date of First Use Anywhere>

<Date of First Use in Commerce>

~*Submit one (1) SPECIMEN for each international class showing the mark as used in commerce.*~

PTO Form 1478 (REV 12/99)
OMB Control No. 0651-0009 (Exp. 8/31/2001)

U. S. DEPARTMENT OF COMMERCE/Patent and Trademark Office
There is no requirement to respond to this collection of information unless a currently valid OMB number is displayed.

Trademarks

Trademark Application – TEAS

<Intent to Use: Section 1(b)>~*Applicant has a bona fide intention to use or use through a related company the mark in commerce on or in connection with the below-identified goods and/or services (15 U.S.C. § 1051(b)).*~
<International Class Number(s)>
<Listing of Goods and/or Services>~*List in ascending numerical class order. Please see sample in HELP instructions.*~

<Foreign Priority: Section 44(d)>~*Applicant has a bona fide intention to use the mark in commerce on or in connection with the below-identified goods and/or services, and asserts a claim of priority based upon a foreign application in accordance with 15 U.S.C. § 1126(d).*~
<International Class Number(s)>
<Listing of Goods and/or Services>~*List in ascending numerical class order. Please see sample in HELP instructions.*~

<Country of Foreign Filing>
<Foreign Application Number>
<Date of Foreign Filing>

<Foreign Registration: Section 44(e)>~*Applicant has a bona fide intention to use the mark in commerce on or in connection with the below-identified goods and/or services based on registration of the mark in applicant's country of origin.*~
<International Class Number(s)>
<Listing of Goods and/or Services>~*List in ascending numerical class order. Please see sample in HELP instructions.*~

<Country of Foreign Registration>
<Foreign Registration Number>
<Foreign Registration Date>
<Foreign Registration Renewal Date>
<Foreign Registration Expiration Date>
~*Submit foreign registration certificate or a certified copy of the foreign registration, in accordance with 15 U.S.C. §1126(e).*~

<FEE INFORMATION>

$325.00 x <Number of Classes>	= <Total Filing Fee Paid>

< SIGNATURE INFORMATION>

~Applicant requests registration of the above-identified mark in the United States Patent and Trademark Office on the Principal Register established by Act of July 5, 1946 (15 U.S.C. § 1051 et seq.) for the above-identified goods and/or services.

The undersigned, being hereby warned that willful false statements and the like so made are punishable by fine or imprisonment, or both, under 18 U.S.C. § 1001, and that such willful false statements may jeopardize the validity of the application or any resulting registration, declares that he/she is properly authorized to execute this application on behalf of the applicant; he/she believes the applicant to be the owner of the trademark/service mark sought to be registered, or, if the application is being filed under 15 U.S.C. § 1051(b), he/she believes applicant to be entitled to use such mark in commerce; to the best of his/her knowledge and belief no other person, firm, corporation, or association has the right to use the mark in commerce, either in the identical form thereof or in such near resemblance thereto as to be likely, when used on or in connection with the goods/services of such other person, to cause confusion, or to cause mistake, or to deceive; and that all statements made of his/her own knowledge are true; and that all statements made on information and belief are believed to be true.~

~Signature~_____

<Date>

<Name>

<Title>

<CONTACT INFORMATION>

<Name>

<Company/Firm Name>

<Street>

<City>

<State>

<Country>

<Zip/Postal Code>

<Telephone Number>

<Fax Number>

<e-Mail Address>

The information collected on this form allows the PTO to determine whether a mark may be registered on the Principal or Supplemental Register, and provides notice of an applicant's claim of ownership of the mark or bona fide intent to use the mark in commerce. Responses to the request for information are required to obtain the benefit of a registration on the Principal or Supplemental Register. 15 U.S.C. §§1051 et seq. and 37 C.F.R. Part 2. All information collected will be made public. Gathering and providing the information will require an estimated seventeen to twenty-three minutes. Please direct comments on the time needed to complete this form, and/or suggestions for reducing this burden to the Chief Information Officer, U.S. Patent and Trademark Office, U.S. Department of Commerce, Washington D.C. 20231. Please note that the PTO may not conduct or sponsor a collection of information using a form that does not display a valid OMB control number. (See bottom left side of this form).

TEAS scannable Form

PTO/TM/1583 (Rev 4/2000)
OMB No. 0651-0009 (Exp. 08/31/2004)

* Declaration of Use of Mark Under Section 8 *
* (15 U.S.C. § 1058) *

* To the Commissioner for Trademarks *

<DOCUMENT INFORMATION>
<DECLARATION OF USE OF A MARK UNDER SECTION 8>
<VERSION 1.22>

<TRADEMARK/SERVICEMARK INFORMATION>
<MARK> E-MUSEME.COM
<REGISTRATION NUMBER> 0999999
<SERIAL NUMBER> 72456955
<REGISTRATION DATE> 11/11/1997

<OWNER INFORMATION>
<NAME> E-MUSE ME,LLC
<STREET> 3333 Entertainment Drive
<CITY> Anywhere
<STATE> CA
<COUNTRY> USA
<ZIP/POSTAL CODE> 44444-4444
<E-MAIL ADDRESS> info@emuseme.com

<GOODS AND SERVICES INFORMATION>
<ALL GOODS AND/OR SERVICES IN EXISTING REGISTRATION> Yes

~ The owner is using or is using through a related company the mark in commerce on or in connection with all the goods/services listed in the existing registration. ~

<FEE INFORMATION>
<SECTION 8 FILING FEE AMOUNT> 100
<NUMBER OF CLASSES> 1
<TOTAL FEES PAID> 100
<NUMBER OF CLASSES> 1

<USE INFORMATION>
<SPECIMEN DESCRIPTION> advertisement

<LAW OFFICE INFORMATION>
<E-MAIL ADDRESS FOR CORRESPONDENCE> info@emuseme.com

~ The USPTO is authorized to communicate with the applicant at the above e-mail address ~

<SIGNATURE AND OTHER INFORMATION>

*~ **Declaration:** The owner is using or is using through a related company the mark in commerce on or in connection with the goods/services identified above, as evidenced by the attached specimen(s) showing the mark as used in commerce. ~*

~ The undersigned being hereby warned that willful false statements and the like are punishable by fine or imprisonment, or both, under 18 U.S.C. §1001, and that such willful false statements and the like may jeopardize the validity of this document, declares that he/she is properly authorized to execute this document on behalf of the Owner; and all statements made of his/her own knowledge are true and that all statements made on information and belief are believed to be true. ~

<SIGNATURE>_____ * please sign here*
<DATE>   _____
<NAME> Mary C. Jones
<TITLE> President

CERTIFICATE OF MAILING
I hereby certify that this correspondence is being deposited with the United States Postal Service with sufficient postage as first class mail in an envelope addressed to:

Assistant Commissioner for Trademarks
2900 Crystal Drive
Arlington, Virginia 22202-3513

on _____
                    Date

_____
                  Signature

_____
Typed or printed name of person
signing certificate

TEAS scannable Form   Page 1 of 2

PTO Form 1963 (Rev 4/2000)
OMB No. 0651-0009 (Exp. 08/31/2004)

* Combined Sections 8 & 9 Declaration/Application *
* (15 U.S.C. §§ 1058 & 1059) *

* To the Commissioner for Trademarks *

\<DOCUMENT INFORMATION\>
\<COMBINED SECTIONS 8 & 9 DECLARATION/APPLICATION\>
\<VERSION 1.22\>

\<TRADEMARK/SERVICEMARK INFORMATION\>
\<MARK\> E-MUSEME.COM
\<REGISTRATION NUMBER\> 0999999
\<SERIAL NUMBER\> 72456955
\<REGISTRATION DATE\> 12/01/1993

\<OWNER INFORMATION\>
\<NAME\> E-MUSE ME, LLC
\<STREET\> 3333 Entertainment, Drive
\<CITY\> Anywhere
\<STATE\> CA
\<COUNTRY\> USA
\<ZIP/POSTAL CODE\> 44444-4444
\<E-MAIL ADDRESS\> info@emuseme.com

\<GOODS AND SERVICES INFORMATION\>
\<ALL GOODS AND/OR SERVICES IN EXISTING REGISTRATION\> Yes

~ The owner is using or is using through a related company the mark in commerce on or in
connection with all the goods/services listed in the existing registration. ~

\<FEE INFORMATION\>
\<COMBINED SECTIONS 8 & 9 FILING FEE AMOUNT\> 1000
\<NUMBER OF CLASSES\> 2
\<TOTAL FEES PAID\> 1000
\<NUMBER OF CLASSES\> 2

\<USE INFORMATION\>
\<SPECIMEN DESCRIPTION\> brochure
\<SPECIMEN DESCRIPTION\> advertisement

\<LAW OFFICE INFORMATION\>
\<E-MAIL ADDRESS FOR CORRESPONDENCE\> info@emuseme.com

~ The USPTO is authorized to communicate with the applicant at the above e-mail address ~

\<SIGNATURE AND OTHER INFORMATION\>

TEAS scannable Form

Page 2 of 2

~ *Declaration: The owner is using or is using through a related company the mark in commerce on or in connection with the goods/services identified above, as evidenced by the attached specimen(s) showing the mark as used in commerce.* ~

~ The undersigned being hereby warned that willful false statements and the like are punishable by fine or imprisonment, or both, under 18 U.S.C. §1001, and that such willful false statements and the like may jeopardize the validity of this document, declares that he/she is properly authorized to execute this document on behalf of the Owner; and all statements made of his/her own knowledge are true and that all statements made on information and belief are believed to be true. ~

~ *Declaration: The registrant requests that the registration be renewed for the goods and/or services identified above.* ~

<SIGNATURE>_____ * please sign here*
<DATE>   _____
<NAME> Mary C.Jones
<TITLE> President

CERTIFICATE OF MAILING
I hereby certify that this correspondence is being deposited with the United States Postal Service with sufficient postage as first class mail in an envelope addressed to:

Assistant Commissioner for Trademarks
2900 Crystal Drive
Arlington, Virginia 22202-3513

on   _____
                Date

     _____
              Signature

     _____
     Typed or printed name of person
     signing certificate

155

TRADEMARK

IN THE UNITED STATES PATENT AND TRADEMARK OFFICE

In the Application of
APPLICANT: CASE NO.:
SERIAL NO.:   TRADEMARK LAW OFFICE:
FILED: TRADEMARK ATTORNEY:
MARK:

RESPONSE TO OFFICE ACTION

Box Responses –
Commissioner for Trademarks
2900 Crystal Drive
Arlington, VA 22202-3513

Sir or Madam:

  In response to the Office Action dated _____, please consider the following:

RESPONSE TO REQUIREMENTS

RESPONSE TO REFUSAL

CONCLUSION

  In view of the foregoing, allowance of the above referenced application is respectfully requested.

         Respectfully submitted,

         Telephone: ( )

156

Dated:_____

Enclosures

Publishing Agreement
Literary Law Guide for Authors
www.LiteraryLawGuide.com

PUBLISHING AGREEMENT

THIS AGREEMENT is made this ___ day of _____, 20__ (The "Agreement"), by and between _____, an individual (hereinafter referred to as "Author") located at _____, and ABC Publishing Company, a corporation (hereinafter referred to as "Publisher") whose principal place of business is located at _____, concerning a work presently entitled _____ (as described in greater detail below).

WHEREAS Author seeks to create a book tentatively titled _____ (the "Work");

WHEREAS Publisher seeks to publish the Work; and

WHEREAS both parties agree to be bound by the terms and conditions set forth in this Agreement,

NOW THEREFORE Author and Publisher agree as follows:

1.   Rights Granted. The Author hereby grants, transfers, and assigns to the Publisher the Work for the full term of copyright the exclusive right to publish in hardback and paperback editions (the "Primary Rights") and to sell throughout the world in the English language. The Author also grants and assigns to the Publisher the subsidiary rights to the Work, with exclusive authority to license said rights in all countries and in all languages. The Author hereby reserves all rights not expressly granted to the Publisher.

[NOTE: This is a broad grant of rights to the publisher that may not be in the best interest of the author. This paragraph should be carefully reviewed and negotiate perhaps to limit the editions, the territory, and the subsidiary rights (sub rights) granted.]

2.   Delivery and Acceptance of the Manuscript.

(a)   Author shall deliver to Publisher on or before _____, 20__ (the "Delivery Date"), one (1) original hard copy of the complete Work and one (1) copy on computer disk, together with any supplementary materials (including, without limitation, drawings, illustrations, photographs, maps, graphs, tables). If Author fails to deliver the Work by the Delivery Date, after a thirty (30) day grace period (or such other time period as shall be determined by the Publisher and agreed to in writing by both parties), Publisher may demand the return of all sums paid to or on behalf of Author by Publisher in connection with the Work, and this Agreement shall terminate. Upon termination under these circumstances, Author may not resubmit the Work (or any part thereof) or a similar work to any other publisher without first offering it to Publisher under the same terms contained in this Agreement.

(b)   Publisher shall inform the Author in writing as to whether the complete Work is acceptable to Publisher in form and content within ninety (90) days of receipt of the complete Work. If Publisher determines the Work is unacceptable but capable of cure, Publisher and Author shall agree upon a time for revision (the "Revision Period")

157

and Publisher shall provide to Author written comments explaining the necessary revisions. If Publisher determines that the first submission cannot be cured or that the revision created during the Revision Period is still unacceptable, Publisher shall have the right, in Publisher's sole discretion, to reject the Work by giving written notice to the Author. If the Work is rejected, Author shall keep fifty percent (50%) of the advances paid to date and shall return the remaining fifty percent (50%) within one year of rejection. The Author may submit the Work to a third party, provided that Author shall remain obligated to repay to Publisher the amounts retained by Author from all proceeds from any sale or license by the Author of rights of any nature in the Work to a third party (the "First Proceeds").

3.   Supplementary Material.

(a)   The Author will prepare, or cause to be prepared, and deliver to the Publisher within ___ weeks of the receipt of page proofs an index to the Work acceptable to the Publisher, unless the parties agree that an index will not be needed.

(b)   If permissions to use copyrighted work in the Work are necessary, the Author shall obtain such permissions at the Author's own expense (after consultation with the Publisher) and shall file them with the Publisher at the time the manuscript is delivered (or as agreed to prior to Delivery). Publisher acknowledges that the permissions request form attached hereto as Exhibit A shall be sufficient evidence, when fully and properly executed, of permission.

[NOTE: Attach a copy of the Permissions Request Form]

4.   Representations and Warranties.

(a)   The Author warrants that he/she is the sole owner of the Work and has full power and authority to make this agreement, and that the Work does not infringe the copyright in any other work, violate the rights to privacy or publicity of any person, or constitute a defamation against any person.

(b)   Publisher represents and warrants that it is a company duly organized, validly existing, and in good standing under the laws of its jurisdiction of charter, having all requisite power and authority to enter into this Agreement, and that it will make no additions or changes to the Work that infringe the copyright in any other work, violate the rights to privacy or publicity of any person, or constitute a defamation against any person.

5.   Duty to Publish.

(a)   The Work shall be published by the Publisher in the English language as soon as circumstances permit after acceptance of the completed manuscript, but in no event later than eighteen (18) months after acceptance, at its own expense, in such style or styles and at such price or prices as the Publisher shall deem best suited to the sale of the Work.

(b)   The Author will bear the expense of any alterations made in the proofs by the Author (exclusive of printer's or Publisher's staff errors) which exceed ten percent (10%) of the cost of the composition.

6.   Artistic Control. The Publisher, in consultation with the Author, shall make all artistic decisions.

7.   Royalties. The Publisher shall pay to the Author on each copy of the Work sold by the Publisher, the following royalties based on the Net Sales of the Work ("Net Sales" being defined as sales, less returns, at list price less trade discounts):

(a)   Hardback: __% on the first 5,000 copies; __% on the next 5,000 copies; __ on all copies thereafter.

(b)   Paperback: __% on the first 10,000 copies; __% on all copies thereafter.

(c)   Mass Market: __% on the first 150,000 copies; __ % on all copies thereafter.

(d)   On hardback and/or paperback copies sold at special discount of 60% or more from the list price, a royalty of __% of the amount the Publisher receives, except as provided in paragraph 16.

(e)   On hardback and/or paperback copies sold for export (outside the United States and Canada), 75% of the royalties stipulated in paragraphs 8(a) - (c), except as provided in paragraph 16.

(f)   No royalty shall be paid on copies furnished without charge for review, advertising, sample, promotion or other similar purposes, or on damaged copies or Author copies.

[Optional Net Revenue Scheme: The net amount of any compensation received from such dispositions will be divided equally between the Author and the Publisher (after all manufacturing costs, commissions, foreign taxes, and other charges) in lieu of royalty, except that the division of the net proceeds from dramatic, motion picture, and television licenses shall be __% to the Author and __% to the Publisher.]

8.   Subsidiary Rights. The Publisher shall have the sole right to license, sell, or otherwise dispose of the following rights in the Work: publication or sale by book clubs; reprint rights; foreign rights; translation rights; publication in anthologies, compilations, digests, condensations; first and second serial rights (in one or more installments); dramatic, motion picture, and television rights; broadcast by radio; recordings; electronic, mechanical, and visual reproduction; computer programs; microprint, microfiche, and microfilm editions; syndication rights; permission rights (quotations, excerpts, illustrations, etc.); any other rights to the Work not specifically enumerated; and otherwise utilize the Work and material based on the Work.

159

[NOTE: This is an all-inclusive sub-rights clause and may not be in an author's best interest. A competent professional should carefully and vigorously negotiate this clause.]

9.   Accounting and Payments. The Publisher shall render to the Author in June and December of each year a biannual statement of account as of the preceding six (6) month period, which shall signal the close of the preceding accounting period. The statement shall show for that period and cumulatively to date the number of copies (1) printed and bound, (2) sold and returned for each royalty rate, (3) distributed free for publicity purposes, (4) remaindered, destroyed, or lost, as well as the royalties paid to and owed to the Author, and licensing income. Payment shall be made within thirty (30) days of the close of the applicable accounting period in US dollars. If the Publisher sets up a reserve against returns of books, the reserve may only be set up for the four accounting periods following the first publication of the Work and shall in no event exceed fifteen percent (15%) of royalties due to the Author in any period.

10.   Inspection of Books.   Author, along with Author's legal or financial representative, shall, upon giving written notice to Publisher or Publisher's designee, have the right once per year to inspect the Publisher's books of account to verify the accounting. If errors in any such accounting are found to be to the Author's disadvantage and represent more than five percent (5%) of the payment to the Author pursuant to said accounting, the cost of the accounting shall be paid by the Publisher. In any case, such payments owed to Author shall be payable immediately.

11.   Copyright.   Publisher shall in all versions of the Work published by Publisher under this Agreement, place a notice of copyright in the name of the author (ex: © 2003 by Patsi Pen) in a form and place that Publisher reasonably believes to comply with the requirements of the United States copyright law, and shall apply for registration of such copyright(s) in the name of the Author in the United States Copyright Office. Publisher shall have the right, but not the obligation, to apply for registration of copyright(s) in the Work published by Publisher elsewhere in the world. Author shall execute and deliver to Publisher any and all documents which Publisher deems necessary or appropriate to evidence or effectuate the rights granted in this Agreement, including but not limited to the Instrument of Recordation. Nothing contained in this Section shall be construed as limiting, modifying or otherwise affecting any of the rights granted to Publisher under this Agreement.

12.   Indemnity. Author and Publisher (each an "Indemnifying Party") hereby agree to indemnify and hold each other harmless from and against any and all claims, demands, actions and rights of action (including reasonable attorneys' fees and costs) which shall or may arise by virtue of: (i) anything done or omitted to be done by the Indemnifying Party (through or by his agents, employees or other representatives) outside the scope of, or in breach of the terms of, this Agreement; (ii) any breach of warranty or representation contained herein; and (iii) any misrepresentation, omission or inaccuracy in any schedule, instrument or paper delivered or to be delivered hereunder or in connection with the transaction herein contemplated.

13.   Author Copies. The Publisher shall give to the Author, free of charge, ___ copies of each edition of the Work as published. Author may purchase additional copies from Publisher for personal use (not for resale) [alternate clause: which Author may resell, at Author's discretion,] at the best available discount, without royalty to the Author. Publisher may deduct the cost of said additional copies from Author's account in lieu of actual payment by Author for such copies.

14.   Revisions. The Author shall revise the Work (a "Revised Work") ___ times after initial publication and within one (1) year upon the receipt of written request from the Publisher to do so. A Revised Work shall not substantially alter the original Work, and further shall not constitute a new work for [copyright and] royalty escalation purposes. In the event that the Author is unable or unwilling to provide a revision within one (1) year after the Publisher has requested it, or should the Author be deceased, the Publisher may have the revision made at the Publisher's expense (such expense to be recoupable from royalties) [and may display in the revised Work and in advertising the name of the person or persons who perform the revision.]

15.   Out-of-Print, Reversion. If the work goes out of print in all Publisher's editions, Author shall have the right to request that Publisher reprint or cause a licensee to reprint the Work. Publisher shall have six (6) months after receipt of any such written request from Author to comply, unless prevented from doing so by circumstances beyond Publisher's control. If Publisher declines to reprint the work as described above or if Publisher agrees to reprint the work but fails to do so within the time allowed, then Author may terminate this Agreement upon thirty (30) days' written notice. Upon such termination, all rights granted under this Agreement, except the rights to dispose of existing stock as set forth in paragraph 16 below, shall revert to Author, subject to all rights which may have been granted by Publisher to third parties under this Agreement, and Publisher shall have no further obligations or liabilities to Author except that Author's earned royalties shall be paid when and as due. Except as provided elsewhere in this Agreement, the work shall not be deemed out of print within the meaning of this section so long as the work is available for sale either from stock in Publisher's, a distributor's or a licensees' warehouse, or in regular sales channels.

[Special clause to address electronic versions of the Work: If Publisher sells no more than _____ copies of Author's Work in either electronic or downloadable format, or by means of print-on-demand technology, over any _____ consecutive month period of this Agreement, then either party may terminate this Agreement upon thirty (30) days' written notice sent to the other party. Upon such termination, all rights granted under this Agreement, except the rights to dispose of existing stock including but not limited to electronic, printed, or audio copies, shall revert to Author, subject to all rights that may have been granted by Publisher to third parties under this Agreement, and Publisher shall have no further obligations or liabilities to Author except that Author's earned royalties shall be paid when and as due.]

16.   Remaindering. If Publisher shall determine that there is insufficient demand for the Work to enable the Publisher to continue its publication and sale profitably, the

Contracts

Publishing Agreement

Publisher may dispose of the copies remaining on hand as it deems best. In such event, Author shall have the right, within ___ days of receiving written notice from Publisher (Notice of Intent to Remainder), to a single purchase of some or all of such copies at the best available discount, and the purchase of film and plates at Publisher's actual cost of manufacture. If Author declines to purchase such copies, Publisher may dispose of such copies, and shall pay Author a sum equal to ten percent (10%) of the amounts actually received by Publisher.

17. <u>Promotion of the Work</u>. The Publisher may publish or permit others to publish or broadcast without charge and without royalty such excerpts from the Work for publicity purposes as may benefit the sale of the Work. Further, the Author consents to the use of his/her name and likeness to promote and advertise the work; provided such use is dignified and consistent with the Author's reputation.

18. <u>No-Compete Clause</u>. The Author agrees not to publish or furnish to any other publisher, without the Publisher's written consent, during the term of this agreement any work on the same subject and of the same content and character as the Work covered by this agreement, publication of which would, in the Publisher's opinion, clearly conflict with the sale of the Work.

19. <u>Options Clause</u>. The Publisher shall, within _____ (__) days from the date of publication, have the option to acquire Author's next book-length work [of [insert genre]] [relating to _____] [on the same terms has set forth hereunder] [on terms to be mutually agreed upon by the parties].

20. <u>Amendments</u>. The written provisions contained in this agreement constitute the sole and entire agreement made between the Author and the Publisher concerning this Work, and any amendments to this agreement shall not be valid unless made in writing and signed by both parties.

21. <u>Notice Provisions</u>. Where written notice is required hereunder, such notice, as well as royalty statements and copies of payments to be made hereunder, shall be given or made to the respective party at the addresses in the recitation.

A copy of all notices to Author shall also be sent to:

Author's Agent
Company
Address
Phone:
Fax:
Email:

Author's Attorney
Firm
Address

Phone:
Fax:
Email:

22. <u>Arbitration</u>. All disputes arising under this agreement shall be submitted to binding arbitration and shall be settled in accordance with the rules of the American Arbitration Association. Judgment upon the arbitration award may be entered in any court having jurisdiction thereof.

23. <u>Construction, Governing Law, Binding Effect, and Assignment</u>. This agreement shall be construed and interpreted according to the laws of the State of _____ and shall be binding upon the parties hereto, their heirs, successors, assigns, and personal representatives.

24. <u>Entire Agreement</u>. This represents the entire agreement between the parties. All modifications must be in writing and signed by both parties.

IN WITNESS WHEREOF, the parties have duly executed this agreement as of the date first written above.

By: [Name of Publisher]

Signatory	Author
Title/Position	Address
Address	City, State Zip
City, State Zip	Social Security Number

163

Work-for-Hire Agreement
Literary Law Guide for Authors
www.LiteraryLawGuide.com

WORK MADE FOR HIRE AGREEMENT
BY AND BETWEEN

_____

AND

_____

THIS AGREEMENT is made by and between _____, a [insert type of entity] located at _____ (hereinafter referred to as "OWNER"), and _____, a [insert type of entity], located at _____ (hereinafter referred to as "you" or "your").

TERMS

This Work-Made-For-Hire Agreement when signed by OWNER and you will confirm the following as our mutual understanding and agreement:

1.   In consideration of the total sum-certain amount of _____ dollars ($_____), you agree to create, provide to and perform for OWNER the specially ordered work and services, referred to below, on a Work-Made-For-Hire basis, as defined under Section 101 of the 1976 Copyright Act, as amended, and on the terms and conditions hereof, to be a supplemental work for OWNER's trade publication, namely [insert title], or for any other uses. All rights of copyright (namely the right to reproduce, to prepare derivative works, to distribute copies, to display the work publicly (or to refrain therefrom), as well as the right of attribution and the right of integrity, and other rights to the specially ordered work and services will vest in OWNER. You obtain no rights of copyright, no right to further compensation, nor any other property or equitable rights in the specially ordered work and services, or in the work in which it is used.

2.   To the extent the rights, including copyright, to the specially ordered work and services do not automatically vest in OWNER, you hereby transfer and assign to OWNER all such rights, including world-wide copyright and renewal rights. Such transfer and assignment is coupled with an interest and is therefore irrevocable. Further, you understand and agree the OWNER reserves the right to terminate your work and services before completion. If so terminated, OWNER will retain all rights to the work as state above, and you shall be entitled to a fair and reasonable portion of the above stated compensation, based upon the amount of work and/or services provided by you to OWNER. You also acknowledge that although it is OWNER's intention to publish _____, to the extent the book is not published and/or released, your supplemental work for the book remains the property of OWNER.

3.   You represent and warrant to OWNER, its successors, designees, licensees and transferees (all hereinafter referred to as "USER") that all items and materials, including without limitation, visual images and designs, writings, dialogue, other copyrightable

Work-for-Hire Agreement
Literary Law Guide for Authors
www.LiteraryLawGuide.com

works, and ideas, created and provided by you to OWNER hereunder, will not obligate USER to make payment to any other party, nor violate the right of privacy or publicity of any person or party, nor constitute a libel or slander against any person or party, nor infringe upon the trademark, service mark, trade dress, copyright, literary, dramatic, artistic, intellectual, or other legal equitable rights of any person or party. You agree that OWNER may use your name and identity in connection with the work and services, and you shall [shall not] receive credit on all copies of _____ and any promotional materials in which your supplemental works appear.

4.   You understand that the information provided to you, used and created by you, and that which becomes known by you in connection with your work and services for OWNER, which includes ideas, concepts, art, audio-visual, and written materials from which you will be working, is to be treated by you as proprietary, trade secret, and confidential information of OWNER. You warrant that you will not discuss or use such information separate of your services rendered, and without OWNER's prior written approval.

5.   This specially ordered work and services you will create and provide to OWNER, which duties you cannot assign are: _____. The due dates for the work and services will be decided upon by mutual agreement in accordance with the publication schedules of OWNER. The due dates set forth and agreed upon are incorporated by reference and made a part of this Agreement.

6.   You agree to return to OWNER or OWNER's designee, all copyrightable works, and elements thereof, information, and materials relating thereto that were provided to you, obtained by you, and that were developed and created hereunder, within twenty-four (24) hours of the last day of work and services, or as otherwise indicated in writing by OWNER or OWNER's designee. Furthermore, you agree to assert no lien against or otherwise cause the materials and rights of OWNER to be encumbered. OWNER's initial designee hereunder is _____, located at _____. Additional or successor designees may be named.

7.   You represent and warrant that you have the full right and authority to enter into this Agreement; you have not made any contract, agreement or commitment in conflict with this Agreement, nor know of any potential conflict that would interfere with or prevent the use of the work and your services; and that you agree to indemnify OWNER and USER for breach of any and all above representations and warranties. You also agree that the warranties made, rights obtained, and duty of indemnification shall survive the termination or completion of the work and services under this Agreement. Lastly, you acknowledge that you have been advised that you have the right to seek outside legal counsel and/or advice from your management representative regarding the terms of the Agreement.

165

Work-for-Hire Agreement
Literary Law Guide for Authors
www.LiteraryLawGuide.com

The undersigned have read, understand and approve this Agreement, and indicate acceptance by signing in the space below.

<u>AGREED AND ACCEPTED:</u>

[OWNER COMPANY]

_____
Name

By: _____

_____
Signature

_____
SSN

_____
Date

Collaboration Agreement
Literary Law Guide for Authors
www.LiteraryLawGuide.com

COLLABORATION AGREEMENT
BY AND BETWEEN

_____

and

_____

THIS COLLABORATION AGREEMENT ("Agreement") is entered into as of the _____ day of _____, 20 _____, (the "Effective Date") between _____, a [enter capacity], located at _____ (hereinafter referred to as "Collaborator 1") and _____, a [enter capacity], located at _____ (hereinafter referred to as "Collaborator 2") regarding a project presently titled [insert working title of the project] ("Work").

TERMS

1.   Description of the Work. The Work shall be approximately _____ words on the subject of _____. Materials other than text shall include _____.

[NOTE: Consider attaching a synopsis or outline of the Work and any other contributions to the Work.]

2.   Term. The term for this Agreement shall be the duration of the copyright, pursuant to the Copyright Act, in effect on the Effective Date, as extended by any renewals or extensions thereof (the "Term").

3.   No Agency. The parties to this Agreement are independent of one another, and nothing contained in this Agreement shall make a partnership, agency, or joint venture between them.

4.   Collaboration. Each party agrees to cooperate with the other as joint authors of the Work, to share equally in all tasks and responsibilities as may be necessary to complete the Work, and to secure its publication and other exploitation, including research, writing and editing of the Work. However, in order to clarify the respective duties of each party, the responsibilities shall be divided as follows:

168

Collaboration Agreement
Literary Law Guide for Authors
www.LiteraryLawGuide.com

(a)   Collaborator 1 shall be responsible for [include this collaborator's responsibilities and what, if any, supplementary materials he/she will supply.]

(b)   Collaborator 2 shall be responsible for [include this collaborator's responsibilities and what, if any, supplementary materials he/she will supply.]

(c)   This Agreement shall remain in effect for the duration of the Term (unless otherwise terminated before such time), and shall be binding upon each party's heirs and successors. However, in the event of the death or disability of either party that will prevent completion of his or her respective portion of the Work, or of a revision thereof or a sequel thereto, the other party shall have the right to complete that portion or to hire a third party to complete that portion and shall adjust the authorship credit to reflect the revised authorship arrangements. The deceased or disabled party shall receive payments pursuant to Paragraph 5 pro rata to the proportion of his or her work completed or, in the case of a revision or sequel, shall receive payments pursuant to Paragraph 5 after deduction for the cost of revising or creating the sequel with respect to his or her portion of the Work. In that case, the active party shall have the sole power to license and contract with respect to the Work, and approval of the personal representative, heirs, or conservator of the deceased or disabled party shall not be required. If all parties are deceased, the respective heirs or personal representatives shall take the place of the parties for all purposes.

(d)   Each party shall complete his or her contribution to the Work by _____, 20 ___, or by the date for delivery of the manuscript as specified in a publishing agreement entered into pursuant to Paragraph 12 below (the "Due Date"). In the event either party fails to complete his or her contribution to the Work by the Due Date, subject to subparagraph (c) above, a reasonable extension of time may be agreed to, or, in the alternative, the parties may agree to allow the non-defaulting party to complete the Work as if the defaulting party were deceased or disabled.

5.   Division of Income and Expenses. Income and expenses generated by or on behalf of the Work shall be divided as follows:

(a)   *Division of Income.* Net Income, defined as gross income as reduced by reasonable expenses, shall be divided equally between the parties [or insert other payment provisions] and paid directly to each party (or his or her designee). If either party receives income payable to the other party, the receiving party shall make immediate payment to the other party of such amounts as are due hereunder.

(b)   *Division of Expenses.* Expenses to produce the Work shall be divided

Collaboration Agreement
Literary Law Guide for Authors
www.LiteraryLawGuide.com

equally between the parties [or insert other expense provisions]. Each party shall provide written proof of expenses and maintain a proper accounting of such expenses and corresponding payments. Unless otherwise provided, the parties' expenses shall be reimbursed from the first proceeds received, including but not limited to advances.

6.   Artistic Decisions.

        (a)   Each party shall have artistic control over his or her portion of the Work. [Artistic control of the entire Work shall be exercised by _____.]

        (b)   The parties shall share ideas and make their work-in-progress available to the other to facilitate completion of the Work. Except as otherwise provided in this Agreement, neither party shall at any time make any changes in the portion of the Work created by the other party without their consent.

7.   Business Decisions.

        (a)   All editorial, business and other decisions affecting the Work, which require consent, shall be made jointly by the parties, and no agreement regarding the Work shall be valid without the signatures of both parties. The parties agree to reasonably consult with each other on such matters, and agree not to unreasonably withhold such consent to any decisions or agreements. In the event that the parties cannot mutually agree, the ultimate decision will be made by [_____].

        (b)   Each party agrees that any communication by him or her to or from any editor, publisher or other industry professional, including an agent so long as both parties are represented by the same agent, must be promptly provided in a detailed manner by mail, fax, or e-mail to the other party.

8.   Copyright, Trademarks and Other Proprietary Rights.

        (a)   The parties agree that the work of each contributor shall be copyrighted in the names of each respective party and that upon completion of each party's contribution, such contributions shall be merged into a joint work with a jointly owned copyright.

        (b)   It is further agreed that trademarks, rights in characters, titles, and similar ongoing rights (collectively referred to as "Proprietary Rights") shall be owned jointly and equally by both parties.

Collaboration Agreement
Literary Law Guide for Authors
www.LiteraryLawGuide.com

9.   Derivative Works.

(a)   No derivative work based on the Work (as defined by the Copyright Act, as revised) shall be developed, created or exploited without the equal participation of each party. However, if either party declines to participate in such a derivative work, then the other party shall be free to go forward on his or her own, and the non-participating collaborator shall be entitled to receive out of any Net Income of such derivative works, one-half (1/2) of the amount that would have been payable to the non-participating collaborator if the derivative work had been jointly prepared.

(b)   Material of any and all kinds developed or obtained in the course of creating the work shall be [jointly owned] [the property of the party who developed or obtained it].

10.   Agent. [The parties have entered into an agency agreement with respect to the Work with the following agent:_____.] The parties agree to seek an agency agreement [not to seek an agency agreement]. Any agency contract shall be mutually acceptable to and entered into in the names of and signed by each party, each of whom shall comply with and perform all required contractual obligations.

11.   Publisher; Licenses. [The parties have entered into a publishing agreement with respect to the Work with the following publisher:_____.] The parties agree to seek a publishing agreement [not to seek an publishing agreement]. Any publishing agreement shall be mutually acceptable to and entered into in the names of and signed by each party, each of whom shall comply with and perform all required contractual obligations.

If a mutually agreeable publishing contract for initial publication of the Work is not entered into with a publisher by _____, 20_____, then both parties shall have the option to:

(a)   Jointly self-publish the Work and to enter into a separate publishing agreement to set forth the terms and conditions thereof.

(b)   Terminate this Agreement, pursuant to the procedures set forth in paragraph 13. Each party shall fully inform the other party of all negotiations for such a publishing agreement or with respect to the negotiation of any other licenses or contracts pursuant to this Agreement. The disposition of any right, including the grant

Page 4 of 7

170

Collaboration Agreement
Literary Law Guide for Authors
www.LiteraryLawGuide.com

of any license, shall require written agreement between both parties. Each party shall receive a copy of any contract, license, or other document relating to this Agreement.

12.　Authorship Credit. The credit line for the Work shall appear as follows wherever authorship credit is given in the Work or in promotion, advertising, or other ancillary uses:_____.

13.　Termination. Except as provided in paragraph 4(c) above, the parties agree to follow the following procedures, if necessary, to terminate this Agreement:

　　　(a)　If any party withdraws from the collaboration before the final manuscript of the Work is fully completed and accepted for publication for publisher, or, in the case of a self-published Work, if the Work has gone to print (the "Withdrawing Party"), then the rights of the Withdrawing Party (including but not limited to the rights to copyright and financial participation, if any) shall be determined by written agreement signed by all parties, or, if such an agreement cannot be reached, pursuant to the terms of paragraph 16 below.

　　　(b)　If the parties determine that they are unable, for any reason, to complete the Work despite their best efforts to do so, then they will submit to arbitration as provided in Paragraph 16 below, to determine the rights and responsibilities of each party at that time to terminate the collaboration efforts fairly and amicably.

14.　Representations and Warranties; Indemnity. Each party warrants and represents to the other that his or her respective contribution(s) to the Work are original (or that appropriate permissions have been obtained) and do not libel or otherwise violate any right of any person or entity, including but not limited to rights of copyright, publicity, or privacy. Each party indemnifies and holds the other harmless from and against any and all claims, actions, liability, damages, costs, and expenses, including reasonable legal fees and expenses, incurred by the other as a result of the breach of such warranties, representations, and undertakings.

15.　Assignment. This Agreement shall not be assignable by either party hereto, provided, however, that after completion of the Work, either party may assign the right to receive income pursuant to Paragraph 5 by giving written notice to the other party.

16.　Arbitration. All disputes arising under this Agreement shall be submitted to confidential binding arbitration and shall be settled in accordance with the rules of the American Arbitration Association. Judgment upon the arbitration award may be

171

Collaboration Agreement
Literary Law Guide for Authors
www.LiteraryLawGuide.com

entered in any court having jurisdiction thereof.

17.   Jurisdiction. This Agreement shall be governed by the laws of the State of

_____.

18.   Non-Disclosure and Non-Competition.

(a)   Each party agrees to hold in trust and confidence all material and information disclosed by one party to the other in connection with the Work, and not to disclose any such material or information to any third party without the prior written consent of the other. All such information and materials shall be regarded as proprietary trade secrets jointly owned and controlled by both parties.

(b)   Each party agrees not to prepare, or to participate in the preparation of, any other work that directly competes with or injures the sales of the Work during the Term without the signed written consent of the other party, such consent not to be unreasonably withheld.

19.   Infringement. In the event of an infringement of the Work, the parties shall have the right to sue jointly for the infringement and, after deducting the expenses of bringing suit, to share equally in any recovery [or insert other recovery provisions]. If either party chooses not to join in the suit, the other party may proceed and, after deducting all the expenses of bringing the suit, any recovery shall be shared between the parties as follows: _____.

20.   Entire Agreement. This Agreement shall be binding upon the parties hereto, their heirs, successors, assigns, and personal representatives. This Agreement constitutes the entire understanding between the parties. Only an instrument in writing signed by both parties can modify its terms. Further, a waiver of any breach of any of the provisions of this Agreement shall not be construed as a continuing waiver of other breaches of the same or other provisions hereof.

21.   Miscellaneous Provisions. Each party shall do all acts and sign all documents required to effectuate this Agreement.

Collaboration Agreement
Literary Law Guide for Authors
www.LiteraryLawGuide.com

IN WITNESS WHEREOF, the parties hereto have signed this Agreement as of the date first set forth above.

_____   _____
[Collaborator 1]   [Collaborator 2]

SSN: _____   SSN: _____

Agency Agreement
Literary Law Guide for Authors
www.LiteraryLawGuide.com

SURE THING AGENCY, INC.
AGREEMENT

THIS AGENCY AGREEMENT ("Agreement") is entered into as of the _____ day of _____, 20 _____, (the "Effective Date") between PATSI PEN, an individual, located at [enter complete address], (hereinafter referred to as the "Author"), and SURE THING AGENCY, INC., a corporation located at [enter complete address], (hereinafter referred to as the "Agent"), as follows:

TERMS

1. <u>Rights; Term</u>. The Author hereby engages Agent, and Agent accepts such engagement, for a term of ___ years, as of the Effective Date, as the Author's sole and exclusive agent and representative throughout the world, unless specifically limited herein, with respect to the Author's services, activities and participation in the literary publication field and the sale, lease, license or other use or disposition in any and all media now or hereafter known (hereinafter "disposition") of all book-length literary works of non-fiction and fiction, unless specifically excluded herein, (hereinafter "properties") created by the Author or owned and/or controlled by the Author or any firm or corporation owned and/or controlled by the Author. The rights herein represented by Agent include, without limitation, electronic publication, foreign publication and foreign language publication, audio recording, motion picture, television, audio-visual media, stage and all merchandising, commercial tie-up and subsidiary rights now or hereafter known relating thereto and all services rendered by the Author in connection with the exploitation of any such rights.

[NOTE: Above is a comprehensive rights clause that may not be in a writer's best interest. Therefore, include, if appropriate, limitations on the rights granted to the agent if, for instance, you want the agent to represent only fiction, or only nonfiction etc. Also include, if appropriate, limitations on the term, territory, and/or media]

2. <u>Representations and Warranties</u>. The Author warrants and represents that the Author has the right to enter into this Agreement and that the Author does not have, nor will the Author hereafter enter into any agreement or incur any obligation in conflict herewith. The Agent warrants and represents that it will market the Author's properties, use its best efforts to negotiate the best available terms and conditions on Author's behalf, and will use its best efforts in the foregoing for the purpose of securing deals based upon the exploitation of Author's properties.

3. <u>Commission</u>.

    a. The Author agrees to pay Agent as and when received by the Author, or on the Author's behalf, or by any person, firm or corporation owned and/or controlled by the Author, directly or indirectly, or in which the Author now has or hereafter during the term hereof acquires any right, title or interest, and Agent agrees to accept, as and for Agent's compensation, a sum equal to

Page 1 of 4

174

Agency Agreement
Literary Law Guide for Authors
www.LiteraryLawGuide.com

Fifteen Percent (15%) of the gross compensation and/or other consideration earned [in the United States and Canada] [throughout the world {delete b.}], whether during or after the term hereof, and without deduction of any kind, pursuant to any contract negotiated during the term of this Agreement, and any and all extensions, renewals, modifications, substitutions for and additions to such contracts whenever made, and whether procured by Agent, the Author or any third party.

b. [In lieu, however, of said Fifteen Percent (15%), Agent's compensation shall be Twenty Percent (20%) with respect to: (i) printed publications in countries other than the United States and Canada; (ii) merchandising, testimonials and commercial tie-up rights and licensing of such rights; and (iii) amateur stage rights.]

c. [Agent may act as packaging agent on projects involving properties and charge its customary packaging fees to third parties. Agent shall not deduct commission from the Author's compensation derived from such package if Agent actually is paid such packaging fees.]

4. <u>Power of Attorney</u>. The Author agrees to authorize and direct that all payments to the Author or on the Author's behalf from engagements covered by this Agreement shall be made to and in the name of the Sure Thing Agency. Inc., as the Author's agent. Agent is hereby authorized (a) to collect all gross compensation and other consideration payable to the Author from engagements covered by this agreement, and (b) to endorse the Author's name to checks, drafts, choses in action and money payable in connection herewith, and deduct therefrom all commissions, loans and other monies due Agent from the Author and thereafter Agent shall remit any sums remaining as the Author shall direct within seven (7) days [5 business days] of receipt of any compensation covered by this Agreement.

5. <u>Conterminous/Co-Extensive Provisions</u>.

a. The term hereof shall match the duration of and be automatically extended and re-extended with respect to any specific engagement, property or material whenever and so long as any contract or contracts covered by this Agreement (as hereinafter defined) relating to such specific engagement, property or material, shall be or continue in effect, including any and all exercises of options, extensions, renewals, modifications, substitutions for and additions to such contract(s), and for one (1) year thereafter.

b. "Contracts covered by this Agreement" means any and every agreement, oral or written, directly or indirectly related to or connected with the disposition or the refraining or the withholding from or limitation upon the disposition of any property or any part thereof or any right or interest therein, covered by this Agreement, whether procured or negotiated by Agent, the Author or any third

Contracts

Agency Agreement

Agency Agreement
Literary Law Guide for Authors
www.LiteraryLawGuide.com

party, whether any such agreement is now in existence or is made or negotiated or to become effective during the term hereof (or within six (6) months after each term hereof, if any such agreement is on terms similar or reasonably comparable to any offer made to the Author during the term hereof and is with the same offeror thereof or any person, firm or corporation directly or indirectly connected with such offeror); and all agreements, oral or written, substituted for or replacing any such agreement, directly or indirectly, and any modifications, supplements, extensions, additions and renewals of any such agreement or substitutions or replacements thereof, whether made, negotiated or to become effective during or after the term hereof and whether procured or negotiated by Agent, the Author or any third party.

6. <u>Non-Exclusive Agency</u>. Agent may render similar services to others, including (a) owners of properties and/or package shows in which the Author's services, properties and/or materials are used, and (b) owners of older properties and/or materials whether or not the same as, similar to or competitive with the properties and/or materials covered by this Agreement.

7. <u>Assignment Clause</u>. Any assignment of any of the Author's rights covered by this Agreement shall be subject to all of Agent's rights hereunder. Agent may assign this Agreement and all of Agent's rights hereunder to a firm or corporation controlling, controlled by or under common control with Agent or to any firm or corporation affiliated with Agent or a subsidiary wholly owned by Agent, but no such assignment will relieve Agent of Agent's obligations hereunder.

[NOTE: This assignment clause gives an agent broad assignment rights that may not be in an author's best interest in the case where an author's file is assigned to an unfamiliar, unsupportive, or otherwise unfavorable firm. This clause should be reviewed carefully.]

8. <u>Binding Contract</u>. This Agreement shall inure to the benefit of and be binding upon Agent and the Author, the Author's heirs, and Agent's and the Author's respective successors and assigns.

9. <u>Notice of Breach; Termination Provisions</u>. Unless provided for elsewhere in this Agreement, no breach of this Agreement by Agent shall entitle the Author to terminate this Agreement unless within thirty (30) days after the Author learns of such breach, the Author serves written notice to Agent by certified mail, and Agent does not remedy such breach within fifteen (15) days after receipt of such notice.

[NOTE: Negotiate breach and termination provisions carefully because this clause controls when and you get out of a bad deal (or do not get out).]

10. <u>Statement of Account; Accounting</u>.

    a. Agent shall send copies of statements of account received by Agent to the Author when rendered.

176

Agency Agreement
Literary Law Guide for Authors
www.LiteraryLawGuide.com

    b. Agent shall keep the books and records with respect to payments due each party at its place of business and permit Author or Author's professional designee to inspect these books and records at least once per year during normal business hours upon giving reasonable notice.

11. <u>Entire Agreement</u>. This Agreement sets forth the entire agreement between Author and Agent with respect to the subject matter hereof (unless and until a more formal agreement is entered into), and this Agreement may not be modified, waived or added to except in writing signed by both parties.

12. <u>Applicable Law</u>. The laws of the State of _____ shall govern this Agreement, its validity, construction and effect. [Insert arbitration provisions, if applicable]

ACCEPTED AND AGREED TO:

SURE THING AGENCY, INC.   PATSI PEN, Author

By: _____   _____

Title:_____   SSN: _____

177

Contracts

License Agreement

Licensing Agreement
Literary Law Guide for Authors
www.LiteraryLawGuide.com

LICENSING AGREEMENT
BY AND BETWEEN

_____

and

_____

THIS LICENSING AGREEMENT is entered into as of the _____ day of _____,
20 _____, (the "Effective Date") between _____, a [enter capacity],
located at _____ (hereinafter referred
to as the "Licensee") and _____, a [enter capacity],
located at _____(hereinafter referred to as the "Licensor") with
respect to the licensing of certain rights in the Licensor's creative work(s) (hereinafter
referred to as the "Property").

TERMS

1.   Description of Property. The Licensee wishes to license certain rights in the
Property that the Licensor has created and/or owns and which is described as follows (as
further described in Exhibit A attached hereto):

[NOTE: Be very specific when describing the Property, using title, word count, subject matter and
copyright information or any other information which helps to identify the Property being licensed
with particularity. Also list any other materials to be provided along with the Property, as well as the
form in which it shall be delivered.]

2.   Delivery Date. The Licensor agrees to deliver the Property on or before
_____, subject to Paragraph 3.

3.   Grant of License. Upon receipt of full payment pursuant to Paragraphs 8 and 9
below, Licensor grants to the Licensee the following [nonexclusive] [exclusive] rights in
the Property: for use as_____ in the _____ language for the
[product] [publication] [purpose] tentatively titled _____.
[For magazine, newspaper or similar contribution: For one-time North American serial
rights].

4.   Term. The term of this Agreement will begin on the Effective Date and will
end one (1) year thereafter. This Agreement will automatically renew each year for an
additional term of one (1) year ("Automatic Renewal"), unless and until either party
notifies the other in writing at least thirty (30) days prior to Automatic Renewal that it
does not wish to renew this Agreement.

Page 1 of 7

Licensing Agreement
Literary Law Guide for Authors
www.LiteraryLawGuide.com

5. <u>Territory</u>. [Worldwide.] [United States.] [North America.]

6. <u>Other Limitations</u>. This Agreement shall be limited by the following additional terms: _____.

[EX: If payments to be made hereunder fall to less than $____ for ____ consecutive months, all rights granted will without further notice revert to the Licensor without prejudice to the Licensor's right to retain sums previously paid and collect additional sums due.]

7. <u>Reservation of Rights</u>. All rights not expressly granted hereunder are reserved to the Licensor, including but not limited to all rights in preliminary and supplementary materials [and all electronic rights. For purposes of this agreement, electronic rights are defined as rights in the digitized form of works that can be encoded, stored, and retrieved from such media as computer disks, CD-ROM, computer databases, and network servers.]

8. <u>License Fee</u>. Licensee agrees to pay the following fee for the license granted herein:
   A. $_____ [if flat fee – state installment schedule, if any]

   B. An advance of $_____ to be recouped against royalties to be computed as follows: [insert royalty schedule]

9. <u>Payment Terms</u>. Licensee agrees to pay the Licensor in US currency [insert payment terms (ex: monthly, quarterly, biannually, on the 1st and 15th)]. Overdue payments shall be subject to interest charges of ___ percent (__%) in each month the overdue payment remains outstanding.

[10. <u>Statements of Account</u>. (Only include if there is a royalty schedule or installment payments)

   A.   The payments due pursuant to Paragraph 8 shall be made by Licensee to Licensor (or Licensor's designee) and shall be accompanied by a statement that includes the amount of and reason for the payment, bank information (if necessary), title and identifying information (ex: ISBN) of the applicable work to which the payment relates, the applicable payment period, and the details of any withholdings for taxes, commissions etc. If Licensee complies with these requirements, Licensor's receipt of the payment shall be a full and valid discharge of the Licensee's obligations hereunder.

   B.   Further, Licensee shall render to Licensor a statement of account

Licensing Agreement
Literary Law Guide for Authors
www.LiteraryLawGuide.com

regarding all revenues received in exploitation of any and all rights granted herein, and all credits and debits relating thereto, and pay to Licensor any amount(s) then owing on the last day of each quarter during the fiscal year beginning January 1 and ending December 31 (March 31, June 30, September 30 and December 31).]

11.   Other Uses of Property. If Licensee wishes to make any additional uses of the Property, Licensee shall request permission from the Licensor and make any such payments as are agreed to between the parties at that time.

12.   Alteration of Property. Licensee shall not make or permit any alterations, whether by adding or removing material from the Property, without the permission of the Licensor. Alterations shall be deemed to include the addition of any illustrations, photographs, sound, text, or computerized effects.

13.   Copyright Notice. Copyright notice in the name of the Licensor shall [shall not] accompany the Property and any related advertising and promotional materials when it is reproduced.

14.   Credit. Credit in the name of the Licensor shall [shall not] accompany the Property and any related advertising and promotional materials when it is reproduced.

15.   Indemnification. The Licensee agrees to indemnify and hold harmless the Licensor, and Licensor's affiliates, officers, directors, employees, consultants and agents, against any and all claims, costs, and expenses, including attorney's fees, due to uses for which no release was requested, uses which exceed the uses allowed pursuant to a release, or uses based on alterations not allowed pursuant to Paragraphs 7 and 12.

[Alternate Provision: Licensor and Licensee each indemnify and hold the other harmless from and against any and all claims, actions, liability, damages, costs, and expenses, including reasonable legal fees and expenses, incurred by the other as a result of the breach of such warranties, representations, and undertakings.]

16.   Confidentiality.

        A.   Confidential Information is defined as information about the disclosing party's business that is proprietary and confidential, which shall include all business, financial, technical and other information of a party marked or designated by such party as "confidential" or "proprietary," or information which, by the nature of the circumstances surrounding the disclosure, ought in good faith to be treated as confidential.

Page 3 of 7

Licensing Agreement
Literary Law Guide for Authors
www.LiteraryLawGuide.com

B.   Each party will:

(i) not disclose to any third party or use any Confidential Information disclosed to it by the other except as expressly permitted in this Agreement; and

(ii) take all reasonable measures to maintain the confidentiality of all Confidential Information of the other party in its possession or, which will in no event be less than the measures it uses to maintain the confidentiality of its own information of similar importance.

C.   Notwithstanding the foregoing, each party may disclose Confidential Information as follows:

(i) to the extent required by a court of competent jurisdiction or other governmental authority or otherwise as required by law; or

(ii) on a "need-to-know" basis under an obligation of confidentiality to its legal counsel, accountants, banks and other sources and their advisors.

D.   The terms and conditions of this Agreement will be deemed to be the Confidential Information of each party and will not be disclosed without the written consent of the other party.

17.   Termination.

A.   Either party may terminate this Agreement if the other party materially breaches its obligations hereunder and such breach remains uncured for thirty (30) days following the notice to the breaching party of the breach.

B.   All payments that have accrued prior to the termination or expiration of this Agreement will be payable in full within thirty (30) days thereof.

C.   The provisions of this Section 17 (Termination), Section 16 (Confidentiality), Section 15 (Warranty and Indemnity), and Section 18 (Arbitration) will survive any termination or expiration of this Agreement.

18.   Arbitration. All disputes arising under this Agreement shall be submitted to binding arbitration before _____ in the following location _____ and settled in accordance with the rules of the American Arbitration Association. Judgment upon the arbitration award may

Page 4 of 7

Licensing Agreement
Literary Law Guide for Authors
www.LiteraryLawGuide.com

be entered in any court having jurisdiction thereof. Disputes in which the amount at issue is less than $_____ shall not be subject to this arbitration provision.

19.   Assignment. Neither party may assign this Agreement, in whole or in part, without the other party's written consent (which will not be withheld), except that no such consent will be required in connection with a merger, reorganization or sale of all, or substantially all, of such party's assets. Any attempt to assign this Agreement other than as permitted above will be null and void.

20.   Governing Law. This Agreement shall be governed by the laws of the State of _____.

21.   Notice. Any notice under this Agreement will be in writing and delivered to the other party by personal delivery, express courier, confirmed facsimile, confirmed email or certified or registered mail, return receipt requested. Notices will be sent to a party at its address set forth above and as follows:

Licensor's Attorney

[Insert information]

Licensee's Attorney

[Insert information]

22.   No Agency. The parties are independent contractors and will have no power or authority to assume or create any obligation or responsibility on behalf of each other. This Agreement will not be construed to create or imply any partnership, agency or joint venture.

23.   Severability. Should any provision of this Agreement be void or unenforceable for any reason, such provisions shall be deemed omitted or modified to the extent required by law and this Agreement with such provisions omitted or so modified shall remain in full force and effect.

24.   Entire Agreement. This Agreement shall be binding upon the parties hereto, their heirs, successors, assigns, and personal representatives. This Agreement constitutes the entire understanding between the parties. Its terms can be modified only by an instrument in writing signed by both parties. A waiver of a breach of any of the provisions of this Agreement shall not be construed as a continuing waiver of other breaches of the same or other provisions hereof.

182

Licensing Agreement
Literary Law Guide for Authors
www.LiteraryLawGuide.com

IN WITNESS WHEREOF, the parties hereto have signed this Agreement as of the date first set forth above.

<u>ACCEPTED AND AGREED TO</u>:

[Licensor]   [Licensee]

_____   _____

Licensing Agreement
Literary Law Guide for Authors
www.LiteraryLawGuide.com

EXHIBIT A

PROPERTY DESCRIPTION

Permission Request Form
Literary Law Guide for Authors
www.LiteraryLawGuide.com

PERMISSION REQUEST FORM

The Undersigned hereby grants permission to _____,
(hereinafter referred to as the "Author"), located at _____, and
to the Author's successors and assigns, to use the material specified in this
Permission Form (hereinafter referred to a "Material") in the book titled
_____ (the "Work") to be published by
_____.

1.   The Material.

      A.   Title and/or nature of Material: [Insert].

      B.   Exact description of Material: [Insert].

      C.   Source of the Material: [Insert].

2.   Publication Information.

      A.   The Material has [has not] been previously published.

      B.   [If published, include copyright notice and ownership information.]

3.   Grant of Rights. Author, or Author's designees, shall have the irrevocable
right to use the Material in the Work and in any future revisions, editions, and
electronic versions thereof, including nonexclusive world rights in all languages. It is
understood that the grant of this permission shall in no way restrict republication of
the Material by the Undersigned or others authorized by the Undersigned.

[Alternate Clause: Grant of Rights Author, or Author's designees, shall have the
exclusive and irrevocable right to use the Material in the Work and in any future
revisions, editions, and electronic versions thereof, including nonexclusive world
rights in all languages.]

4.   Copyright Notice and Credit. On publication the Material shall be
accompanied by a copyright notice as follows: _____ and a
credit line as follows: The _____ is reproduced from [inert
name/description of material], by _____ © [date] by _____.
Used with the permission of the [publisher/author], _____.

5.   Miscellaneous Provisions. [Insert other provisions, if any:

Permission Request Form
Literary Law Guide for Authors
www.LiteraryLawGuide.com

_____.]

6.   Ownership.   The Undersigned warrants that he/she has the exclusive right to grant permission to use the Material.

[Alternate insert: The Undersigned does not have the exclusive right to permit use of the Material and permission must also be granted by the following owners: _____.]

AGREED TO AND ACCEPTED:

_____   _____
[Name]   Date

Business Name:_____

Business Address:_____

City, State Zip:_____

Business Telephone:_____ Fax:_____

E-mail:_____

Website:_____

186

Page 2 of 2

Glossary

acceptance A publisher's approval of a delivered manuscript (or other item to be delivered).

author Generally a writer, but in the context of the Copyright Act, it includes anyone who creates an original work.

assignment Transfer of copyright ownership from one person or entity to another.

attribution, right of Ensures that artists are properly identified with the works of art they create and that they are not identified with works they did not create.

automated database A body of facts, data, or other information assembled into an organized format suitable for use in a computer and comprising one or more files.

Berne Convention An international copyright treaty that requires all signatories to eliminate formality requirements as a condition of copyright protection. But the formality requirements eliminated by amendment remain important because works created after 1978, the enactment date of the act of 1976, but before 1989, when the act of 1976 was revised and when the United States signed the Berne Convention, are governed by the first version of the 1976 act.

bundle of rights All of the individual rights conferred by copyright: namely the right to copy, distribute, prepare derivative works, display, and perform publicly.

collaboration agreement An agreement between two or more people who contribute work to a book or other creation.

collective works Defined in the Copyright Act as "a number of contributions, constituting separate and independent works in themselves . . . assembled into a collective whole." Individuals or entities who combine individual contributions into one collection hold the copyright in the collection as a whole. But the individual authors retain right to the individual work apart from the collection. This limitation is found in section 201(c) of the Copyright Act: "In the absence of an express transfer of the copyright or of any rights under it, the owner of the copyright in the collective work is presumed to have acquired only the privilege of reproducing and distributing the contribution as part of that particular collective work, any revision of that collective work, and any later collective work in the same series." Thus, other than the rights to reproduce and distribute the collection, and the right to create a derivative work of the collection, the individual contributors to the collection retain the copyright to their individual contributions.

common law A body of law that is made up of cases rather than laws enacted by legislation.

consideration A legal concept best described as the benefit or detriment that induces someone to make a promise and enter into a contractual arrangement based on the terms, conditions, rights, and obligations agreed to by the parties involved.

copies According to the Copyright Act, material objects, other than phonorecords, in which a work is fixed by any method now known or later developed, and from which the work can be perceived, reproduced, or otherwise communicated, either directly or with the aid of a machine or device. The term "copies" includes the material object, other than a phonorecord, in which the work is first fixed.

copyleft A play on the word "copyright," used by a few people who have created a movement to oppose what they deem to be an unfair monopoly on creative expression held by copyright owners, particularly in the software industry. This term is not found in the Copyright Act itself. Rather, it was created to challenge established copyright laws. "Copyleft" is used primarily by members of the Free Software Foundation, which promotes GNU, a project designed to provide software that is free from licensing fees or restrictions on use. Richard Stallman started the GNU project in 1983 based on his belief that software should contain a notice and a General Public License that grants reuse and reproduction rights to everyone and requires anyone who uses it to grant the same rights to others.

copyright The exclusive rights of a copyright owner of a work to make and distribute copies, prepare derivative works, and perform and display the work publicly.

copyright registration Submitting the copyrighted work to the Copyright Office, pursuant to the rules and guidelines set forth by that office.

created The fixing of a work in a copy or phonorecord for the first time. When a work is prepared over time, the portion of it that has been fixed at any particular time constitutes the work as of that time; and when the work has been prepared in different versions, each version constitutes a separate work.

damages Generally, a sum of money paid in compensation for loss or injury.

delivery The act of giving the manuscript (or other item to be delivered) to the publisher.

delivery date The stipulated date by which an author must deliver the manuscript to the publisher.

deposit The physical copy or copies that must be submitted along with a copyright registration form.

execute To complete, make valid, or give effect by signing.

fair use A doctrine that permits use of copyrighted materials for certain purposes listed in the Copyright Act, such as criticism, comment, news reporting, teaching (including multiple copies for classroom use), scholarship, or research. While technically infringing on the copyright owner's rights, these uses are considered permissible; and such fair use can be used as a defense against a claim of copyright infringement.

first proceeds The money received by an author from any sale or license of any rights in his or her copyrighted work to a third party (someone other than the company that originally agreed to publish the work). This situation may arise if the publisher and author enter into a publishing contract, the publisher pays the author an advance, and later the publisher rejects the author's manuscript. If the author then sells the work to another publisher, the first publisher may require the author to repay it from the first money payable to the author as a result of the second publishing deal.

independent contractor One who is self-employed and has the right to control the means and methods of performing work.

integrity, right of Allows a visual artist to protect his or her work from modifications or destruction that injures the artist's reputation.

joint work A work prepared by two or more authors with the intention that their contributions be merged into inseparable or interdependent parts of a unitary whole.

legal vetting See vetting.

legalese Expressions used primarily by lawyers to articulate and discuss legal issues.

licensing agreement An agreement that sets forth the terms that allow others the limited right to use your work (or for you to use the work of others). You remain the owner of the copyright. A license can be exclusive (only the licensee can use it) or nonexclusive (the licensee can use your work but cannot exclude others from doing so).

literary works Works, other than audiovisual works, expressed in words, numbers, or other verbal or numerical symbols or indicia, regardless of the nature of the material objects, such as books, periodicals, manuscripts, phonorecords, film, tapes, disks, or cards, in which they are embodied.

Madrid Agreement A treaty that provides for the international registration of trademarks. It was adopted in 1891 at a conference held in Madrid, Spain, and is administered by WIPO (www.wipo.org). It is augmented by the Madrid Protocol, another treaty for the international registration of trademarks.

Madrid Union The organization of all the countries that belong to the Madrid Agreement, which allows U.S. trademark owners to file for registration in any member country by filing a single standardized application, in English, with a single set of fees, at the USPTO.

moral rights Refers collectively to the right of attribution and the right of integrity.

phonorecords Material objects, such as cassette tapes, CDs, or LPs – but not motion picture soundtracks on which sounds are recorded and which combine moving images and sound.

poor man's copyright The myth that if you mail yourself a copy of your work and do not open it, you can use it to establish the date that your work existed in case you ever need to defend your work or challenge a work you believe infringes on your rights. The poor man's copyright does not offer any additional protection beyond that which already exists once your idea is fixed and thus your work is created. Additionally, it does not constitute a registration of your copyright.

primary rights The main set of rights that a publisher intends to exploit. Generally this means the right to publish the work in book form (hard cover and paperback rights, and perhaps book club rights and so forth). Compare with subsidiary rights below.

privacy, right of The right to be left alone. The three generally recognized invasions of privacy include intrusion, unreasonable publicity, and false light.

189

publication The distribution of copies or phonorecords of a work to the public by sale or other transfer of ownership, or by rental, lease, or lending. The offering to distribute copies or phonorecords to a group of persons for purposes of further distribution, public performance, or public display constitutes publication. A public performance or display of a work does not of itself constitute publication.

public domain The total absence of copyright protection in a work. A work in the public domain is available to anyone to copy, distribute, perform, display, make derivatives of, or use as he or she sees fit. The author of a work in public domain has none of the exclusive rights that apply to a copyrighted work. Note that the public domain is not an actual place or database but a term that describes the absence of copyright protection. Furthermore, it does not refer to freeware or shareware. In actuality, free- and shareware are copyrighted software distributed without advance payment.

publicity, right of A person's exclusive right to use his or her name, likeness, or other aspect of his or her persona, and the right to prevent others from using those aspects without authorization.

publisher A person or entity that produces any periodical, magazine, newspaper, book, manual, advertising materials, or other similar material, whether in printed, electronic, or other form.

revision period The period of time a publisher grants to an author to revise a manuscript.

subsidiary rights The secondary set of rights that may be transferred to a publisher. This may include rights that exist as a result of the primary rights, for example, audio, motion picture and TV, dramatic, mass market paperback, and electronic rights. Compare with primary rights above.

vetting A line-by-line review of a manuscript for potential legal issues.

work made for hire A legal doctrine which says that for purposes of copyright protection, the one who commissioned the work to be created by an independent contractor, and not the creator of the work, is the owner of that work; and that an employer owns the copyright to any artistic or literary work that is created by an employee on company time using company equipment.

References

Books

Copyright Law Reporter and *Copyright Law Decisions*. Riverwood, IL: CCH Incorporated, 1978. These companion books focus on cases and analysis, and are geared toward experienced copyright and intellectual property practitioners.

Goldstein, Paul. *Copyright*. New York: Aspen Law & Business, 1996. This four-volume treatise explains fundamental copyright law in a way that nonspecialists can understand.

Guinn, David, and Harold Orenstein. *Entertainment Law & Business: A Guide to the Law and Business Practices of the Entertainment Industry*. Vol. 2. Salem, New Hampshire: Butterworth Legal Publishers, 1989.

Kirsch, Jonathan. *Kirsch's Handbook of Publishing Law*. Venice, CA: Acrobat Books, 1995.

Nimmer, Melville B. *Nimmer on Copyright*. New York: Matthew Bender, 1976. Considered by intellectual property practitioners and judges to be the leading treatise on copyright, this ten-volume set covers every conceivable aspect of copyright law. Not appropriate for non-lawyers.

Stephen, Laura Lee, ed. *The E-Copyright Law Handbook*. New York: Aspen Law & Business, 2002.

Articles

Moore, Schuyler M. "Raising Defenses to Right-of-Publicity Claims." Parts 1 and 2. *Entertainment Law & Finance* 17, no. 6 (2001): 3–4; no. 7 (2001): 3–4.

Web sites

Legal Information Institute of Cornell University:

Contracts	http://www.law.cornell.edu/topics/contracts.html
Copyright	http://www.law.cornell.edu/topics/copyright.html
Damages	http://www.law.cornell.edu/topics/damages.html
Patent	http://www.law.cornell.edu/topics/patent.html
Publicity	http://www.law.cornell.edu/topics/publicity.html
Trademark	http://www.law.cornell.edu/topics/trademark.html
Unfair Comp	http://www.law.cornell.edu/topics/unfair_competition.html

www.freeadvice.com
www.findlaw.com
www.authorsguild.org
www.copyright.gov
www.uspto.gov
www.wipo.org
www.icann.org

(this page is intentionally blank—this type does NOT print)

About the Author

Tonya M. Evans, Esquire, also known as Lawyer by day, Poet by night™, is an attorney and owner of the Philadelphia law firm of TME Law, LLC. She practices in the areas of intellectual property (copyright, trademark, licensing), publishing law, estate planning (wills, trusts), and public finance. Tonya has developed a professional niche within the publishing industry, representing authors in the review and negotiation of publishing and subsidiary rights deals, and educating authors through seminars and workshops on self-publishing and literary law.

Tonya received a B.S. in communication studies from Northwestern University, which she attended on a full four-year tennis scholarship. Thereafter, she played on the women's professional tennis tour for four years, competing most notably at the U.S. Open and Virginia Slims of Philadelphia in 1993.

In 1995, Tonya attended Howard University School of Law. She served as editor-in-chief of the Howard Law Journal and graduated with honors in 1998. She served as law clerk to Judge Theodore McKee in the Third Circuit Court of Appeals and worked at large law firms before joining practice with her mother, and then opening her own law firm. Tonya is a member of the Pennsylvania, New Jersey, District of Columbia, Eastern District of Pennsylvania, and Third Circuit Bars; she also belongs to the Author's Guild and Publishers Marketing Association.

193

Tonya lectures across the country on copyright and trademark law, and on self-publishing and successful negotiations in the publishing industry. She has also written numerous articles and contributed to *Black Issues Book Review* and *QBR: The Black Book Review*. In addition, she is an accomplished poet, performer, and writer. Her books include *And Then One Day She Knew*, *The Blues*, *Seasons of Her*, and *SHINE!*

(this page is intentionally blank—this type does NOT print)

Acknowledgments

Dan Poynter, the publishing guru, went above and beyond the call of duty to help me help myself. I deeply appreciate his assistance, encouragement, advice, and leadership.

With deep appreciation I thank my editor, Lisa A. Smith. Her professionalism and the quality of her work are second to none. I feel privileged to have her on my team because, with her insight and ability, she has helped me to transform my idea into a book that far exceeded my expectations. I thank Rob Roehrick for an interior design that is cutting-edge and top-notch. And thanks to James "True" Jones for an amazing cover design, which Publishers Marketing Association named as finalist in the 2004 Benjamin Franklin Awards. He listened to my nebulous concepts and turned them (almost overnight) into a first-rate cover that pops.

To all who did not support my endeavors in the beginning, my gratitude because they strengthened my resolve to tap into my inner self. To those who did support me (both named and unnamed), many, many thanks because they made me even stronger by reminding me why I do what I do.

And last but not least, thanks to Clarissa Pinkola Estes, who, in her book *Women Who Run With the Wolves*, advised that "all that you are seeking is also seeking you."

(this page is intentionally blank—this type does NOT print)

Index

Books Published by FYOS Entertainment, LLC

Under the FYOS® Publishing Imprint

Poetry

- *Seasons of Her: A Collection of Poetry*
- *SHINE! Inspirational Poetry w/Companion CD*
- *An Old Soul Reborn*
- *Desire True*

Fiction

- *And Then One Day She Knew*
- *The Blues*

Under the LE Series™ Books Imprint

Literary Entrepreneur Series™

Reference Guides for Authors

- *Literary Law Guide for Authors: Copyright, Trademark, and Contracts in Plain Language*
- *FYOS Literary Law Primer*
- *E-Books for Writers*
- *9 Things Every Writer MUST Know About the Law*
- *Writing About Real People and Places: How to Successfully Navigate the Rights of Publicity and Privacy*
- *Using Other People's Words: Fair Use, Permissions, and Work Made for Hire*

(this page is intentionally blank—this type does NOT print)

In Future Editions and Publications from

LE Series™ Books (An FYOS Entertainment, LLC, imprint)

- Case law and legislation updates

- Hot topics in intellectual property (copyright vs. copymonopoly)

- Expanded section on subsidiary rights

- Revised and new forms

- Author Q&A

- A special section for self-published authors

- Expanded commentary for forms

- A special section for freelance writers

- *International Law and the Author*

- *Internet and Electronic Publishing Law*

If you have a topic you'd like to see covered in a future edition, e-mail your question, comment, or topic to info@literarylawguide.com, or visit www.literarylawguide.com.

(this page is intentionally blank—this type does NOT print)

Direct Sales Order Form

For info:	info@fyos.com
Web orders:	www.fyos.com
Fax orders:	215-438-0469. Send this form.
Phone orders:	215-438-0468. Have your credit card ready.
Mail orders:	FYOS Order Fulfillment, P.O. Box 25216, Philadelphia, PA 19119. USA
Bulk orders:	info@fyos.com for discounts and specials for clubs, schools, and organizations
Trade orders:	Trade orders handled by Independent Publishers Group:

        Phone: 800-888-4741
        E-mail: orders@ipgbook.com
        Mail: Independent Publishers Group
                Order Department
                814 North Franklin Street
                Chicago, IL 60610
        Web: www.ipgbook.com

Titles ordered:

Title _____ Quantity _____

Title _____ Quantity _____

Title _____ Quantity _____

Please send me information on the following items:

☐ other books   ☐ speaking/seminars/events/performances   ☐ e-newsletter   ☐ legal services

Name _____

Address _____ City _____ State ____ Zip ____

Phone _____ E-mail _____

Sales tax: Please add 6% for products shipped to Pennsylvania addresses outside of Philadelphia and 7% for Philadelphia addresses.

Shipping: In U.S. $4.50 for the first book, $2 for each additional book. International $10 US for the first book, $5 US for each additional book.

Payment: ☐ Check   ☐ Visa   ☐ MasterCard   ☐ Am Ex

Card number _____ Exp _____ Name on card _____

Billing address (if different from above) _____

1 DISK INCLUDED

Identifying writers' most important legal issues, this invaluable legal reference provides straightforward information and solutions on how writers can protect their work. With specific attention paid to intellectual property, electronic rights, reclaiming copyright, fair use, permissions, work-for-hire, public domain, and trademarks, this resource provides information necessary for those looking to sell and protect their work. The author covers the most recent changes in copyright and trademark laws as well as pending and new legislation affecting writers. The appendix includes contract, copyright, and trademark forms commonly used by authors, which are also available in a PDF format on the accompanying CD-ROM.

"This clear and understandable overview includes practical advice and real-world examples. Recommended for most public libraries."
- *Library Journal*

"Here is a wealth of valuable information in a concise, well-organized package. Don't sign a contract without it!"
- *Jim Barnes, Managing Editor, Independent Publisher Online/Jenkins Group*
www.independentpublisher.com

"...offers excellent information for the author to contemplate as they are offered a contract with a publishing house or literary agent. This book is a must for every author's reference library."
- *Jeffrey Bowen, President & Publisher, PubInsider.com*

"...provides writers with a user-friendly reference that clearly presents the facts they need to know about fair use, public domain, and electronic rights, so that writers can maximize the value of their work and protect themselves from legal attack."
- *Brian Jud, author of Beyond the Bookstore, BookMarketing.com*

"...breaks down complex intellectual law into simple terms authors can understand. We highly recommend this book—it's [...] ffers huge returns."
- *Mack E. Smith and [...]*
Authors of How to S[...] & Market Your Own Book

Literary Entrepreneur Series™

An imprint of FYOS Entertainment, LLC
www.fyos.com

Forms on CD-ROM

U.S. $22.95   Can. $32.95

ISBN 096745797-1

9 790967 457979   52295>